HEARTS ON P

HEARTS ON PILGRIMAGE

The Agony of Life
The Ecstasy of Love
The Triumph of the Spirit

George and Carolyn Mallone

eagle

Guildford, Surrey

Copyright © 1994 George and Carolyn Mallone

British Library Cataloguing-in-Publication Data. A catalogue record for this book is available from the British Library

Published by Highland Books, an imprint of Inter Publishing Service (IPS) Ltd, 59 Woodbridge Road, Guildford, Surrey GU1 4RF.

All rights reserved. No part of this publication may be reproduced or transmitted in any form or by any means, electronic or mechanical, including photocopying, recording or any information storage and retrieval system, without either prior permission in writing from the publisher or a licence permitting restricted copying.

In the United Kingdom such licences are issued by the Publishers Licensing Society Ltd, 90 Tottenham Court Road, London W1P 9HE.

Typeset by Electronic Book Factory, Cowdenbeath.
Printed in the UK by HarperCollins Manufacturing, Glasgow.

ISBN No: 1 897913 06 0

To our children:
Bo, Dee, David
Faye, Scott, Meredyth

You suffered a great loss.
You supported us in our hour of need.
You stood with us in a new marriage.
We will always love you.

APPRECIATIONS

We owe a debt of gratitude to our friends and family who sustained us in our crisis and enabled us to produce this book. Carolyn Boyd was there every step of the way as Carolyn produced her original draft, and Doylene Boese edited the manuscript and encouraged the publication of one chapter.

Glenn Terrell led the church while George was absent with a sick wife. The 'Spurs' believed Carolyn that her word about a future husband was not silly, but worth the effort of prayer. Faye, Scott and Meredyth tolerated romantic newlyweds running around the house. Jack and Pat Godfrey 'connected' Carolyn to a successful business and concerned themselves with her wellbeing.

Donna Bromley, Meredyth's godmother, received the word of George's remarriage with faith and welcomed Carolyn into a friendship. Elliott Johnson pastored Hugh and Carolyn and gave his blessing for the new phase of her life. Jeff and Tracy Kirby wept over our agonies, and rejoiced in our blessings, and led us in our marriage vows.

Bo, Dee, Kevin, David, Jean and the entire Driggers family stepped up when Hugh died, offering Carolyn their support, finances, and encouragement. Barbara, Kathie, Melinda, and Nancy managed shifts during Bonnie's illness, allowing George time to recuperate. Our mothers, Lexie and La Velle, themselves both widows, blessed the marriage from the start.

Our new daughter-in-law, Kim, used her editing skills

and made many helpful corrections to the first draft. When singles are normally excluded from the ranks of couples, Carolyn was welcomed by the Lingards, Bennetts, Winters, Vaughns, Talkingtons, and Hunns. The congregation of the Grace Vineyard warmly received Carolyn into their midst as a friend and counselor.

Paddy Ducklow, Ken Blue, Bob Birch, Terry Lamb, Jeff Kirby and Glenn Terrell have always been available for George, either to cry or laugh and sometimes, to raise a coherent theological thought. And for all the 'singles,' who know like Carolyn the 'shark-infested waters,' take heart – nothing is impossible with God! Last, but not least, thanks to Penny and Kathryn Wilemon for listening to God and arranging our first date.

Sola deo gloria!

CONTENTS

	Appreciations	7
	Foreword by Anne Watson	11
	Preface	13
1	'Dad is Gone!'	15
2	'One Week to Live!'	21
3	Preparation Road	28
4	'I Will Break You, But I Will Use You!'	41
5	Crisis in Circumstances	53
6	'O Lord . . . Give Me Success'	61
7	More Than a Love Story	66
8	The Christian Assumption	80
9	Two Little Pilgrims, Walking Down the Road of Life	82
10	No Pain, No Gain!	87
11	He is There, And He is Not Silent	100
12	'Living by Faith in a Fallen World'	114
13	Overs	122
	Notes	126

FOREWORD

The first time I read the manuscript of this book I was sitting in a beautiful garden enjoying the warmth of a Texas spring. George and Carolyn had invited me to stay in their lovely home – Carolyn is very gifted artistically – while I was speaking in various Vineyard churches. We had such fun together. My late husband, David, and I had first met George in Canada a number of years before, with his first wife Bonnie and their children, Faye and Scott. Meredyth was still a thought in God's heart. Over the years letters have been exchanged and David and I benefited greatly from reading George's books. When Bonnie first became ill I remember the anxiety we felt for her. Although the Mallones were so far away it seemed they lived just round the corner. Bonnie's valiant fight against the recurring nature of her illness was an inspiration to many people, not least when it came to our turn to enter the valley of the shadow of death. For George and Bonnie the valley was long and winding with occasional breaks of sunshine: for David and myself it was much shorter. David passed into glory ahead of Bonnie and I prayed more earnestly that she would live. I knew the peaks and troughs of emotion that George would be experiencing and prayed for strength for him and the church.

When George, Faye and Meredyth visited Fiona and me on their way to take Faye to Scotland for her first term at university, we talked openly and freely. We laughed and cried as we shared our common experiences. So many people had wanted to know about David's death from my point of view – especially publishers. But here was an occasion when it really was appropriate to talk. I prayed again that Bonnie would be alive when they returned. I knew the dichotomy of wanting rest and peace on the one hand and the awfulness of loss on the other.

When the news of Bonnie's death arrived I felt the release of her spirit but also the awful pall of separation that George must be experiencing which I knew so well. It was time to pray again. Meredyth needed a mother and George a wife. When news came of God's answer I was overjoyed. I met Carolyn at the Pastor's Conference in Anaheim last year. Here was a woman to gladden the heart of any man. And she was such fun to be around. It was not until I read her story in Texas this spring that I realised that the beauty I saw had been honed and fashioned by suffering. Here was a woman whose faith had expanded in a 'severe test of affliction', not shrivelled to make her bitter and complaining. Carolyn's tenderness and sensitivity to Meredyth were helping her to face what was such a major crisis so early in her life. As you will read, God's sign of the blooming bulbs was so easy for a child to understand.

Their story is a testimony that 'many waters cannot quench love' especially the love that God has for the sons and daughters of men.

Anne Watson
Yorkshire
July 1994

PREFACE

Over the last decade I have written a number of small paperbacks for the Christian community. In these I had a chance to expound upon personal spirituality and the renewal of the church. Owing to some unusual pastoral experiences along the way, I thought someday I might attempt a short story, telling both the humorous and tragic tales of my ministry. However, I was never prepared for the circumstances that would overwhelm my life and lead me to the words you are about to read.

Hearts on Pilgrimage, as the title suggests, is a story of agony, ecstasy and triumph. How Carolyn and I lived through all of it, and why we are fortunate enough to be able to tell you what we learned, is beyond our comprehension. There are still things we do not know, and we don't expect to understand them until our life is over. But we have been given some insight on how to run the race of life, the kind of information that enables us to joyfully put one foot in front of the other.

This book will be particularly helpful if you define yourself as a 'babyboomer,' one who was born shortly after the end of World War II. Our generation has lived in the expanding bubble of the happy consumer. Now, we await a rather ominous future and watch how sufficiently we have reproduced our values in our children. It is now that we have begun to experience the awkwardness of our decaying bodies and to see the names of friends listed in the obituary column. It is now that we have begun to worry about the stability of Social Security and health provisions for our future. We are mortal and our time is coming to an end! Such a prognosis naturally produces a certain amount of fear. How will we survive if we have to undergo a prolonged illness? How will we endure the loss of a mate? What would we do if all our economic benefits ceased to exist? How will we face death when it looks us square in the face?

Carolyn and I have had to wrestle with each of these questions already and, graciously, we have been given sufficient help by God to keep on living with purpose. It is our hope that you will be inspired by our story and motivated to place personal confidence in the God we have come to know; the God of the living and the dead.

April 11, 1993
Easter Sunday
Our First Anniversary

1
'DAD IS GONE!'

CAROLYN

March 13, 1987 Months had gone into the planning of our family ski trip to Colorado. Although we had been with our friends in Utah in January, this trip was to be for the children and our one grandchild. My husband, Hugh, decided at the last minute to fly our daughter, Dee, our grandson, Austin and myself to Denver. He felt it would be easier on us and the baby. So plans were made for Hugh, our two sons, and our son-in-law to leave Friday night. They would take two cars and pick us up at Stapleton Airport (Denver) the following evening. The week had been busy, getting ski gear together, preparing food for the week and gathering games for our evenings' entertainment.

The afternoon before we left, I was cleaning up leaves in the front yard when my next-door neighbor walked by. She was on her way home after helping another neighbor clean her yard.

'What does it take to get your help in cleaning a yard?' I asked her humorously. Innocently, she replied, 'You have to become a widow.' Well, that left me out! So I continued with the chores at hand, dismissing our short conversation from my mind.

The next morning, I dressed and went to a neighborhood Bible study. When I arrived, one of the ladies rushed over to me and said, 'I woke up at two o'clock this morning thinking about you and prayed for you the rest of the night. How are you feeling? What's happening in your life right now?'

To my knowledge, everything was fine, but I was grateful for her concern and prayer.

Later that afternoon, the departure time had come. Both cars were packed, and the guys were chomping at the bit to get on the road. Hugh was the happiest man in the world as he drove out of the driveway, smiling from ear to ear. Austin had given his granddad a big hug, and now he was headed to the mountains with all his kids for a week of skiing.

I spent the night at my daughter's house, eagerly anticipating our departure the next day. It was a chatty evening as Dee and I prepared for bed. We were sitting on the sofa, toe to toe, giggling when the phone rang. Dee rushed to pick it up, hoping not to disturb Austin. 'Hello,' she said in a hushed tone. Then there was a long silence before I heard phrases like, 'It can't be. They were just here. You must be mistaken.' I sensed that something was wrong and went to check. She stared at me in disbelief, her color ashen. 'There's been a car accident. Dad is gone!'

Hugh Edwards Driggers Jr.

Hugh Driggers was the first of four children born to a small-town Arkansas family. His father owned and operated a large laundry business, while his mom stayed at home to raise the kids. From his early days at the University of Oklahoma, Hugh wanted to be a Navy pilot, but a bad back forced him into a career as an aeronautical engineer. We met during his last year at the university and decided to get married in the spring, after graduation. For twenty-nine years we raised children, launched a successful engineering career, and relished life. Hugh was tender, patient, loyal, helpful, a good listener, and a strong, quiet leader. He was full of energy, athletic in his appearance, and able to fix almost anything and teach you how it worked. Raised a Baptist, his faith became personally real to him later in life, and it became obvious to everyone that his priority was the kingdom of God. He was my best friend, and now he was gone.

Hugh died in a one-car accident on a small farm-to-market road in northeast Texas. He was driving and was killed instantly. Bo, our oldest son, was the only passenger and was not injured.

Quite legitimately, other women may have screamed through tears, or articulated denial at the notice of their husband's death. For me, it was more like emotional paralysis.

In fact, I felt nothing until later that evening. Being the responsible person that I am, my mind was racing with questions of the immediate. How was Bo? Where had they taken Hugh? Where were the other boys who were traveling in the second car? Hugh was gone, and someone needed to be rational for the family at this time.

As was his custom to take care of every detail, Hugh had many years before made plans to donate his body to a 'living organ bank.' So, when the accident occurred, the closest hospital was immediately able to use his body to help others. Since the accident happened on a farm road and was handled by the Highway Patrol, it took hours to get all the details. On our end, we handled the crisis with as few people as possible. At this point we still had not located the second car (the one in which my youngest son, David, and son-in-law, Kevin, were traveling) and had to leave word at the hotel where they had reservations for that evening.

I was grateful to be at Dee's; it gave me solitude when I so desperately needed it. Everyone wanted to visit to comfort me, but that night I needed to turn to God and seek his direction on how to respond to this circumstance. I needed to make myself available to him and not to other people. I vividly remember spending that night lying on the den sofa, looking into the night sky. For the early part of the evening, I acted like a robot. I listened to people talking and responded as coherently as possible. However, nothing seemed real.

It was like a bad dream, and surely I would awaken

soon. At this point there were no tears, no emotion, just doing what had to be done. The children were foremost in my mind and everything else seemed unimportant. Even though it was only a few hours since I had been with Hugh, I began to feel the deep missing and loneliness of a long separation.

The evening progressed into a night of great contrasts. My emotions began to engage once again, fluctuating between immense sorrow and great peace. I remember thinking of Israel's King David, who, in his periods of anger and depression, took great comfort from God when he remembered to take refuge in him (Ps 18; 22). During the night there were periods when I was overcome with my loss, thinking, 'What do I do now? What will become of me? Where will I turn?'

Throughout the night, however, God met my desperation with such heavenly comfort that my heart was overwhelmed with joy. There were times when I was in the pit of despair, only to be swept up as on the wings of an eagle to the very mountain-tops. Somewhere in those very long hours of the night, grief and grace kissed.

No doubt some would have been tempted to anger if they had been in my shoes. I would have felt the same, if it hadn't been for a special infusion of God's grace. Thus, I found myself able to identify entirely with God's interest in my crisis. My senses were heightened; I could see the tragedy without confusion. Supernaturally, I began to see my concerns from God's perspective. His grace became a melody in my spirit, so much so that my soul was filled with joy. The cares of the world were suddenly put into perspective and lost all their power over me. Priorities were ordered and the superficial urgencies held little sway. God's grace was controlling my time and each minute became visible and valuable. There was no rush or waste in this special state of grace, only contentment and order. Tears produced healing, a release of my control and a surrender of my hurting heart. Bitterness, anger, pain and sorrow were swallowed in grace, and replaced by forgiveness, gratefulness, peace and love.

While in this special state, in the early hours of the morning before the world was awake, the Spirit of God also brought me to a new understanding of eternal life and the kingdom of God. I was led in the scriptures to Luke 9:59–60. Here Jesus was walking down a road when a young man came up to him. Jesus said to him, 'Follow me.' The young man replied, 'Let me go and bury my father and then I will follow you.' But Jesus said, 'No, let the dead bury their dead – you follow me and proclaim the kingdom of God.' When Hugh was living on earth, he was with me. I now saw that he was still living, just absent from my view. He was present with the Lord. From that moment on, I never viewed him as dead, I viewed him as alive. My role seemed clear. I was to proclaim the kingdom of God by giving testimony to God's eternal life for Hugh.

Memorial service

March 17, 1987 The day before Hugh's memorial service I had gone to my room to rest and to read some of the comforting notes people had sent. Over the next few years these words, and especially the notes given to me by my share group, provided encouragement to endure the pain. As I sat there, reading and crying, I came across a notice from the bank which said, 'You are overdrawn!' I said, 'Hello, world!' An unwelcome daily reality had knocked on my door in the midst of my grief.

With this distraction, the Lord spoke these words to my mind. 'The world will tell you that you are overdrawn, insufficient and lacking. I tell you, on this day, you have made a deposit and your account is balanced, sufficient and lacking nothing.' I was unsure of the exact meaning of these words, but they were certainly comforting.

During the grieving process, some uttered words like, 'What a senseless loss!'; 'What unfair timing on the part of God!' However, that was not the way I saw the accident at all. I then wondered. 'Could this word from the Lord mean that on the night of Hugh's death,

I had deposited with God the Father my greatest asset?' Without a husband, I saw myself as poor. Was God now saying that I was rich in his kingdom? Was this act of accepting God's plan a deposit of faith to grow spiritually in the darkest hour?

Could I not already sense a peaceful and overflowing joy within? These words of 'promise' meant much more in the weeks ahead. They came as rays of great hope on cloudy days.

The fourth day after the accident, we had a lovely memorial service. It was a celebration of Hugh's life, and hundreds of friends shared their love and sympathy. As with all tragedies that involve Christian believers, people pulled together to see the heavenly purpose behind the events of the week.

To paraphrase my long-time devotional partner, Oswald Chambers, the voice of God is spoken in the language we know best, not through our ears, but through our circumstances.[1] I had now come to a God-ordained crisis of circumstance.

'Dad was gone!'

2

'ONE WEEK TO LIVE!'

GEORGE

August 18, 1991 It was a brief vision, but very clear. Bonnie and I were in Denver, Colorado, attending a conference for Vineyard Christian Fellowship pastors. We had taken special care in planning the trip, since it was to be our last family outing before Faye, our oldest daughter, left for law school in Scotland. Scott and Meredyth would be seeing friends and their days would be full of fun Colorado activities. There was a sense that we might not have many more times together as a family, so we needed to make the most of our trip.

As the week progressed, Bonnie began to feel sick. At first, she could not eat without being nauseated. Later, an all-too-familiar signal appeared; severe pain in her pelvic area. For eight years, Bonnie had battled with ovarian–fallopian cancer. Four surgeries, treatments in Greece and Mexico, and one round of chemotherapy had not stopped the progress of the disease. Now the symptoms were returning. We prayed, but very little happened.

As we worshipped in the conference, I asked the Lord, 'What's going on with Bonnie?' Immediately, I had a vision. I saw a brown Jeep, just like the one we would buy Scott two weeks later. The Jeep was floating down a river and about to go over a waterfall. Disaster seemed imminent. Instead, the canvas top on the Jeep acted like a parachute, keeping it from falling. Gently, the Jeep turned around and headed back upstream. But, as I peered into the car, I realized that there were only four seats available. At that moment, I knew we were about to lose Bonnie.

So, as we drove back to Texas, four years to the date of our arrival in Arlington, I tried to stretch the trip as long as I could. We had traveled thousands of miles together in our Suburban; playing music, picking restaurants and fighting over who got the spare pillows. Now we were taking our last ride as a family.

September 5–8 Bonnie had never conceded death by cancer. She steadfastly fought it in every way she could. So, it was not surprising when she demanded we fulfill a speaking obligation in the interior of British Columbia, Canada. While at the airport before leaving, she ate the smallest bit of a hotdog, chewing it carefully. This tiny amount of food left her feeling so bad that she had to deplane by wheelchair when we arrived. The next day she fought to regain the strength depleted in travel and rallied sufficiently to lead a two-hour workshop on her favorite topic, 'Communicating God to Your Children.'

September 17 Bonnie had several medical tests that day, throwing up as she went. Dale Rank, our compassionate surgeon for three years, called to say that her bowels were obstructed. I was scheduled in two weeks to take Faye to Scotland, so I asked the all-important question, 'How long will she live?' His response was so direct, it took my breath away. 'I don't see how she could live more than a week!'

For the first time, I had hard evidence of my month-long suspicion. Although Bonnie respected Dr Rank, she did not attribute to him god-like powers in pronouncing life and death. She took the information seriously, but carried on with life as usual. That afternoon, I made contact with St Joseph's Hospice, and they graciously began to care for all of our medical needs. There were nurses, social workers, chaplains, grief experts and maids to cover all the bases and over the next ten weeks, these people became intimate members of the family.

That evening, I sat down with the children to explain the situation. As a pastor, I had seen almost every crisis imaginable. I had been called upon to say comforting words, when comfort was not possible. Yet, these words were the hardest I had ever uttered. I held Meredyth in my arms, she then being nine years old, and looked at Faye and Scott as they lay on the floor. My emotions were running wild, and so was my mind. I needed to be strong for the kids, yet I knew I needed to be vulnerable. We were honest in our discussion and with our tears. In the end, I could only utter these words; 'Kids, life is not fair. But, God is good. Somehow, he will show himself to be good to us.'[1] My words were not only theologically correct, but proved to be prophetic.

Over the next two weeks, Bonnie engaged herself in a series of activities. She attended church and watched Scott be baptized. She spoke to the congregation, comforting their fears and giving focus for their lives. She went to Faye's surprise birthday party (her 18th) and spent time with her mother. Her dearest friend Donna Bromley flew in from Canada. They sat together on the bed, hugged one another and cried. It was during these few days that she stopped eating solid food altogether. Nothing would stay down. For fifty-three days, she survived on ice chips alone.

'You take the low road ... I'll be in Scotland before you'

October 1 In the final days of Bonnie's life, I saw numerous heroic gestures. One of the most outstanding, and forever etched on my mind, was Faye leaving her mother to go off to university. Frank discussions had preceded the departure. Under no circumstances would Bonnie allow Faye to withdraw her commitment to law school. The consequences were obvious. Faye would say goodbye to her mother, and never see her again. We had decided that Meredyth and I would still accompany Faye, Donna and Scott remaining at home with Bonnie. The hour of our departure finally came. Faye went to her mother's bedroom to receive a final blessing. Frail, yet still able to walk, Bonnie emerged from the bedroom to see Faye off at the door. She had waved her queenly hand at Faye in her trek from elementary to high school. This last goodbye was stately, believing and full of love. She assured Faye that whether she lived or died, she would be in Scotland before her. As we drove off to the airport, Bonnie confessed to Donna, 'They don't make movies this sad.'

October 12 Somehow Bonnie toughed it out and survived while I was away. She assured me when I arrived home, 'Georgie, I wasn't going to die while you were away!' But during that time, she had begun to throw up every four hours and the pain medication had to be consistently upgraded.

For the next forty-one days, I was the primary caregiver for Bonnie. My sister, Barbara Applequist, Kathie Terrell, Nancy Houston and Melinda Gibson spelled me off from 10:00 a.m. until 2:00 p.m. each day. In those free moments, I slept or did some shopping. Although the routine was hard: up four times a night, giving medicine, carrying her to the portable potty and cleaning out the throw-up bucket – I would not have traded it for the world. It was a time to love her in ways I had not done before. One of my prophetic friends who had seen Bonnie's impending death said that my last days with her would be a honeymoon. That it was. Yet, on particularly bad evenings when there was no sleep, I prayed that it would soon end.

Nightly, we went through our 10:00 pm ritual. Pottytime. Medi-time. Tuck-in time. I slept on the floor at the end of the bed. I would say, 'Good night Joe!' and she replied, 'Good night Joe!' Sometimes I prayed:

> Now I lay Bonnie down to sleep,
> I pray the Lord her soul to keep,
> but if she should die before I wake,
> I pray the Lord her soul to take.

One evening I was concerned that she would not make it through the night, so I said to her, 'Bons, when you are going to go, I want you to tell me.' 'What do you want me to say?' she asked. I told her to say, 'Honey, I'm going now.' 'Honey, I'm going now!' she replied. 'Now?' I cried out. 'No, I'm just practicing,' she teased.

Holy women

November 20 Bonnie's body was now wearing out, and a hospital bed was required for the bedroom. The morphine kept her comfortable, but was beginning to affect her mind and speech. She imagined and heard things no one had said; she even accused me of calling her by the name of my old girlfriend. A yeast infection began to spread in her mouth so that she could not even swallow her ice chips.

For some time, I had heard the Lord telling me to call in the 'holy women' when I knew her death was near (Acts 9:39; 1 Pet 3:5). These would be women who modeled the virtues Bonnie cherished. So seven women gathered that evening around her bed. They prayed, sang, laughed, told stories about Bonnie and had tea together. She loved it, though she could not talk. The following day, though, was hard. Things began to happen to her body that we were not prepared for and did not know how to handle. We stumbled through, laughing and crying at the same time.

With Jesus

November 22 I awoke at 2:00 a.m. and 4:00 a.m. Bonnie's breathing was rough. An hour later, I was up again assuring her that she was home with us and that we loved her. As I got into bed, I was so tired that I cried out to God, 'O, Lord take her home!' Within a minute I heard a 'thump,' as though someone had hit her on the chest. I waited to hear her breathe, but there were no sounds.

This one, designed for heaven, had taken leave of her

body. Previously, she was 'in Jesus,' now she was 'with Jesus.' For the next five hours, the children and I, along with the Applequists and Terrells, spent time in her room loving her and saying our farewells. Frail and exhausted, she still looked beautiful. Alone with her, with tears running down my cheeks, as clear as a bell I heard her speak: 'It will be all right, Georgie.' That proved to be very helpful in just a few weeks time.

As pre-arranged by Bonnie, Glenn Terrell went into the bedroom by himself, and with a back-up team of people praying in various homes, asked the Lord to raise her from the dead. There were no movements. She had already made her way to the Father.

Old friends found the date of her death curious. It was the same day C.S. Lewis had died. In 1963, when the world mourned the death of Jack Kennedy, some devoted followers of another 'Jack' (as Bonnie used to say) quietly observed his passing.

'Why seek the living among the dead?'

November 25 Four carloads of friends and family followed me to Cottage Hill. It was here that generations of my family were laid to rest. Bonnie was buried next to my father, who had died nineteen months earlier. We had sensed Bonnie's spirit with us from the moment she died.

Long-time pastoral friends led the service of committal and joined me at the graveside to sing 'It Is Well With My Soul.' Later in the afternoon, there was a memorial service at the church which went on for several hours, and I did not want it to end. As we left the building, there was the most striking sunset. Certainly it is unprovable, but I had the sense that Bonnie was now leaving us for 'deep heaven with Jesus.' Her spirit had been with us for a few days, but now she was gone.

After the memorial service, we tried to settle into a routine without Bonnie, but the grief was intense. Waves of crying came to each of us at different times – thinking we heard her voice, going to my Mom's for dinner, coming home after school. At the same time, knowing death was hanging over her head, we had been grieving for years.

Even though we missed her deeply, we began to realize that Bonnie was having the time of her life. As one friend said, 'Bonnie wasn't built for earth; heaven has always been her home.' Murray Harris's book *From Grave To Glory* was particularly encouraging.[2] There are many adjectives and prepositions we can use to describe the believer's relationship to Jesus. Most notably is the qualifier 'in Christ' (2 Cor 5:17; 1 Thess 4:16). However, 'with Christ' (Phil 1:23) or 'with the Lord' (2 Cor 5:8) *is never used to describe an earthly experience of a Christian, but only an experience that comes after death.* Bonnie had many spiritual experiences in Jesus, but now she was having the richest time of her life. Bonnie was 'with Jesus.' Who of us would bring her back? Not me! Trust me, I knew the woman for twenty-eight years and she would shoot me if I tried to do so!

Another comforting thought had come to me after returning from Scotland. I was meditating on these words from 1 Corinthians 2:9:

> No eye has seen,
> no ear has heard,
> no mind has conceived
> what God has prepared for those who love him.

Again, I was consoled. I knew how much Bonnie loved Jesus. Now I knew what a great future God intended for her. She taught us to live for Jesus. Now she was teaching us to die with Jesus (Rev 12:11). Maybe there was some truth in the saying, 'Only the good die young.'

3
PREPARATION ROAD

CAROLYN

The roads of life are unexpectedly full of twists and turns. Sometimes they are smooth and level, and other times they are bumpy and full of potholes. Naturally, the road I preferred was the smooth and well-charted one, the one I travelled before Hugh's death and knew well, for it was where I placed my security – in familiarity. Unlike other women who rearranged their furniture every week or so just to experience change, I balanced the furniture for the best design in the room once and *never* moved it again. This was a subtle sign of my 'flexibility.' Even after I became a Christian, I still had a hard time with change and uncertainty. Although I could always adjust, I never seemed to embrace change easily.

Strangely, this all began to shift eighteen months before Hugh's death. It was during this time that I began to notice a drastic difference in my attitudes. Little things that used to throw me into a state of panic suddenly didn't matter. I had a 'So what is the worst thing that could happen?' outlook. This was a special grace to me for, as you can imagine, after Hugh's death my life was a kaleidoscope of change. It was during these eighteen months that I discovered new things about myself and my heavenly Father, revelations which prepared me for the road ahead.

California, here we come?

October, 1985 – November, 1986 We lived in Arlington, Texas, in the same home for twenty years, and

Preparation Road

now suddenly we were preparing for a year and a half move to California. Hugh was a project manager with L.T.V. Corporation, and he had been consumed with one particular program for nearly a decade. So, a year and a half transfer to California sounded like a vacation. I could see how weary he was, and of course I was willing to follow him anywhere. But California? And now!

At this point, I found myself somewhat double-minded. I hated the thought of leaving everything I was familiar with, a new grandson, my three children, and all our closest friends. And what about the Bible study I had been teaching at the fashion college for over two years? The Lord was certainly doing an important work there. And there was 'the Spurs,' my share group. The Lord had uniquely put this group of nine gals together from all over North Texas. Regularly we got together to support each other in our walks with the Lord. I was so blessed by these women; they were not only wonderful, but *wonderfun*! When they heard we were leaving, they arranged a going-away party for us, and then later laughed with us when we did not leave. However, there were benefits of moving to California; I would be near my sister who lived there, and besides, Hugh said we could have a place near the beach.

Potentially, it had the possibility of being a honeymoon at company expense. It began to sound better all the time. However, as often happens in the corporate world, the trip was on one minute and off the next. Eventually, it was cancelled altogether. Due to this experience with uncertainty, I realized I couldn't go back to my previous Texas routine, so I decided to do in Texas what I had planned to do in California.

For over two decades, I had functioned as a wife and mother. I was orderly, but did not have any great goals for myself other than surviving the day with the children and loving Hugh when he returned home. The prospect of moving to California ignited in me a desire to fulfill some personal goals. I knew this would require some discipline and prayer, but I thought they were worth the effort and I would do them in Texas. I wanted to start going places and doing things *alone*. I also wanted to become a good listener and especially one that did not gossip about everything she heard. I began to learn in my share group the value of being a good listener, especially when people knew their words were held in confidence. I planned to work on resisting a judgmental spirit. From time to time, this crept into my heart, and I decided it was time for this unlovely characteristic to go. With these three major areas, there were also a few minor goals. I wanted to learn to spell better, so I decided to write to more people. This came in handy when the Lord spoke to me after Hugh's death and told me to write my story for publication. I also wanted to learn to play tennis and *really* learn the book of Ephesians.

Hugh and I both greeted the news of the cancelled trip as an opportunity to spend more time together, removed from the responsibilities we held in previous years. It was a lovely year, one in which my personal confidence grew and my appreciation for Hugh heightened.

Mom on the slopes

January, 1986 The Driggers family were snowskiing fanatics! They not only loved the sport, but the possibility of a ski trip was often the topic of conversation throughout the year. This possibility became a reality in January when friends invited us to join them at their condominium in Park City, Utah. Three couples would be going, and the six of us had been close friends for many years. Hugh was ecstatic.

To the fans of this sport, sailing freely down a mountain, over the snow-covered peaks and valleys, in a silent wonderland of winter beauty, is heaven! However, my picture of the same scene was extreme cold, unfathomable heights, and uncontrolled speed. Oh, I tried! It looked like great fun, and though others made it appear easy, this was not my experience. To begin with, the equipment resembled relics from a Chinese torture chamber. Frankenstein boots, with long thin planks clamped onto the bottoms, and two long poles with spikes on the ends, did not fit my idea of gear for a romp in the snow! Furthermore, my torso was so bulky with layers and layers of clothing that I looked and moved like a B-movie mummy! The only parts on my body that were flexible or visible were my eyes, and they were wide open with fear. There, I said it, *fear*!

I had faced this word before and discovered that I resolved every major decision in my life out of fear. Isn't that overwhelming! My fear was born out of focus on myself and failure to believe and apply God's word. Now, the principle of faith I understood, but the application was another thing altogether. So God chose snowskiing to expose my fearful heart and pinpointed three arenas, the fear of failure, the fear of falling, and the fear of fainting.

Somehow, in a way I can't explain, God was producing in me a brave new desire, calling me out of the hands of my old enemy. 'OK,' I said to myself, 'the Lord didn't give me a spirit of fear . . . sooooo I will just go on this ski trip and if I don't ski, it will be because I don't like skiing, but not because I am afraid.' Lest you think I went on to join the U.S. ski team, let me assure you that I did not. But I did enjoy the week of skiing, because I was given sufficient courage to overcome all my old fears.

'I have seen your tears!'

March, 1986 As I talked with my friend on the phone, she told me of the Bible study being conducted in her home and about the guest teacher for the week. 'She has the gift of prophecy, so try to come!' My response was less than promising. But, to my surprise, I found myself dressing to go that Friday morning. As I drove to her house, I prayed that the Lord would give me a discerning spirit.

The meeting had begun when I arrived, so I took a seat near the back. The speaker was a pleasant lady in her fifties. Her talk was well-grounded in the scriptures, and she spoke with a gentle authority. She ended her session in prayer, and for a short period, she seemed unconcerned about the group as she prayed quietly. There was a gentle peace around her as she moved about the room. Slowly, she moved toward a lady sitting across the room and spoke directly to her. She addressed a subject which only the women knew, obviously giving her hope with her words.

With my head bowed to the floor, I was startled when she began to pray for me. My heart began beating faster. The thought which flashed across my mind was, 'Why did she come to me? I've never been here before!' I felt her hands gently touch my head with one hand on my forehead and the other on the back of my neck. The silence was deafening; then in a bold, clear voice she began to speak.

'My child, you have loved me. You have been obedient because you love me. I have known your pain and have seen your tears. Because of your obedience, I will put you in high places and I will make your feet like hind's feet.[1] Because you give to others what I give to you, I will continue to fill you and you will continue to give.'

With these uplifting words, I was moved to tears. I couldn't remember all she said, but I knew it was meant for me, and I knew she was anointed to say it.

Exactly one year later, I was suddenly without a husband and a monthly income. But God's word to me was clear. 'I have known your pain and have seen your tears.'

A day of prayer

May 1, 1986 Another day which proved to be very important in my preparation was the National Day of Prayer. I had taken the day to intercede with my friends over the needs facing America. We began our prayer in a large group, but later divided into various rooms of the house to pray alone. I sat on a chair in the middle of a room that was sparsely furnished and was referred to by my hostess as the 'cast-out room.' For some strange reason, I felt very comfortable in the 'cast-out room' because this was a real picture of our Savior, the outcast of his own nation.

After a period of intense meditation, I asked the Lord, 'What do you see?' I was not prepared for what followed. Sentences began to come, and I wrote them as quickly as they appeared on the screen of my mind:

> You are ashamed of me.
> You worship other gods. Materialism.
> You have become proud in your religion.
> You have quenched my Holy Spirit by trying to control him.
> You have perverted my word and your people have become perverted.
> You have stiff necks, puffed-up heads and hard hearts.
> You seek the counsel of the world to become wise in your own understanding.
> You love yourselves and those who agree with you.
> You are motivated by selfish gain and recognition.
> The cells of my body are separated and diseased. There is judgment and unforgiveness. My body will be made whole and complete and lacking in nothing when my church is restored in my righteousness. Turn your faces from the world and focus your spirit on my kingdom.
> My kingdom is balancing the evil in the world. The time grows short.
> You are my kingdom and through you, my body, I will be revealed. You have been given my promises. The time has come for you to claim them and live them. Believe me, stop being deceived by what you think you see. We are one, draw on me! You will see my glory.

My eyes raced over those convicting words, and I realized someone was in big trouble. I knew it couldn't be me because I wasn't any of the things included on the list, but I could see a lot of people to whom these things applied. 'Lord, have mercy on all of these people!' As you can see, my prayer about a judgmental spirit had not been fully answered!

Early the next morning, I took the list out and asked the Lord again, 'Lord, how do you see me in this list?' If you don't ask the question, you don't hear the answer. I asked and I heard. This list was the key to repentance as Christ saw it. He started at the top and showed me that I *was* the list. I never saw myself so clearly, and it broke my heart. Using a whole box of tissues, I wept over each item and realized my crying was from the pain caused by my spiritual condition. In my intense grief, I found great release in God's forgiveness. I had the joy and excitement of a babe in Christ. I had a new hunger to know the promises of God, to dialogue with him about the way he saw everything, but mostly, to just be still and know that he was God. This was to be the beginning of a change in my vision of the kingdom of God.

New York

May, 1986 Although our move to California never materialized, a trip with my sister was taking shape. Jean was a flight attendant, and her flying schedule had given her several lay-overs in New York City. She thought it would be fun for the two of us to go together since I had never been.

As the trip unfolded, Jean asked me to meet her at the airport in Newark, New Jersey. As I made preparations for the trip, the entire family stood with their mouths open in disbelief. *I was about to go on a holiday by myself.* Even though I felt very comfortable with this plan, I realized that, in the past, I had been carefully sheltered from the realities of big city life and also that Hugh had always made the travel arrangements for us.

With my plans settled, horror stories began to surface about women being mugged in New York. Everyone had advice about what to do or not do. It was a real fear situation until I went to my tennis league on Friday. A lady I had not met previously was my match for the following week and I told her we had to reschedule our game because I would be in New York. She was a native New Yorker and encouraged me with these words: 'Don't be afraid of the city, enjoy yourself, you'll be in safe places.' I chose to believe her.

Shortly after this reassurance, something unexpected happened during my prayer time. The Lord impressed upon me that I should pray for his blessings over the city while I was there. I was willing, but I didn't know exactly what he meant for me to do. Needless to say, my sister was relieved when I told her I wouldn't be standing on the street corners crying, 'Repent!'

Everything was progressing flawlessly until four days before the trip, when I sprained my left ankle. The prospect for the trip now looked bleak. The day before my departure, Hugh said the time had come and I had to declare if I was going or not. As I sat with my foot propped up and wrapped in ice, I picked up my daily devotional book and read the selection for the day. The last sentence on the page read, 'Walk before me.' That was it; I was going.

As the Lord had spoken, every place where we walked I called forth his blessing. I asked God's blessing from above the city as we flew over it; from under the city as we rode its subways; through the city as we rode its busses and taxis; and around the city as we viewed it from the top of the Empire State Building. As we did this, we felt God's protection everywhere we went. Native New Yorkers, who are projected as cold and insensitive, were very helpful to us.

In the end, I learned much from the trip. I now had conquered the fear of traveling alone and the fear of being in large and dangerous places. I learned that listening to God is the greatest protection one could ever have. But most important was the realization that, as I stepped out and grasped each new situation, God would meet my every need. Already, I was learning that God was the friend and protector of the orphan and the *widow* [Ps 146:9].

Designing woman

July, 1986 Through the experience of a dear friend, I began to think about what life would be like without a husband. Her world was turned upside down when her husband of thirty years decided to walk away from the marriage. She married young, had four children and became a homemaker. They had always been an active, talented family and probably more involved than anyone else I knew. Yet with the divorce, she lost everything: marriage, leadership in a city-wide Bible study ministry, home, lifestyle, position in the community, and her feelings of self-worth. I didn't dwell on it, but I wondered what I would do if I was ever in those circumstances.

A year or so later, Hugh and I were at a dinner party when the hostess began talking to me about interior decorating. She and her husband had recently moved into a house which needed redecorating and updating. They had been guests in our home and admired our decorating efforts. As she showed me around the house, we exchanged ideas and then she asked if I would help bring the same style to her house. I was flattered and said, 'Yes!' Later in the evening, another guest asked for the same help. On the way home, I asked Hugh if he thought there might be a gap in the decorating business – showing others how to use color, texture and patterns to decorate a space. I had done this all my life as an amateur artist and decorator. It was an area of confidence and interest to me. Hugh, my constant encourager, suggested that I call my friend who owned the real-estate firm and see if this was indeed a need. The next day I called and she confirmed my beliefs, adding that, if I would go into business, she would be my first client. All the lights were green, and within the month I had two clients and a wonderful name for the business, 'Roomscapes.'

During the next year, Hugh and the children took great interest and pleasure in my new little business. Everyday I learned something new and began to grow in greater confidence. During this time, I realized that circumstances have a way of exposing where we are and who we are, along with a clearer understanding of who God is. I would draw on these lessons months later when I was without income and was forced to work full-time. I now see that God used Roomscapes to prepare me to move ahead with confidence.

Not your average camper

October, 1986 'No, you're not going by yourself, I'll go with you!' I could not believe what I had just said. I had volunteered to go camping with my husband! We were both shocked by the announcement. Camping was a special time for the guys and Hugh always said my idea of camping was an unairconditioned motel. He was right! But for some strange reason, I felt prompted by God to volunteer to be Hugh's camping partner. My announcement spoke volumes of love to him.

Our Arkansas campsite sat on a peninsula overlooking the lake; we had a view of the sunset that would rival any sunset in Hawaii. The water was crystal clear with fish jumping to the surface for insects. We set up our camp, built a fire and hung a hammock. As the sun slowly sank into the water, darkness fell and the sky came to life with millions of stars. I could remember lying on the grass as a child on a summer night, looking up and believing the stars were lights shining through the holes in the floor of heaven. I knew this was a week I would remember forever.

We slept in a tent by our fire and fell asleep to the sound of waves lapping at the shore. Daily, we awoke before sunrise. Our perfect little spot had one missing comfort, and it was up the hill and down the walkway. Very clean, but it was not in our tent.

Morning after morning we sat with a hot cup of coffee

and watched the dark hills on the eastern shore of the lake turn pink with the dawn. The water reflected the glow and the waterfowl swept over the lake. There was an indescribable sense of peace. Hugh cooked every meal with the joy and skill of an Eagle Scout. We fished and took long walks along the shoreline and through the rolling, wooded hills. There were no interruptions, and we talked about things we had seldom mentioned – death, remarriage, and choices we would want the other to make.

My husband looked at me differently after our camping trip. He knew camping was not my first choice, but I was willing to do something which made him happy. As I reflected on the trip after Hugh's death, I became aware of the importance of heeding the promptings of God. In obedience, there are no regrets.

A frightening dream

January, 1987 Ski time had come around again, and with our friends we had gathered in Utah for another fun-filled week. Near the end of the week, I had a very disturbing dream. I awoke with a start, almost hysterical, and in tears. Hugh was very comforting and listened as I described the dream. 'Hugh, you called me and asked me to meet you at a model car race. You wanted me to bring a special part, so that you could participate. I rushed to get ready because I did not expect your call, but I got to the race track as fast as I could.' As in many dreams, locations and faces are sometimes confusing. The race was being held on our church property, but the church was gone. I became frantic when I could not find Hugh. Several people I knew came and went, but nobody had seen Hugh. I went from place to place, but he was not to be found. Someone suggested that I try another location, but he was not there either. I was exhausted and traumatized when I finished the dream.

After hearing the dream, Hugh suggested that my old fear of skiing, this time in being separated from one another on two different slopes, may have resurfaced. His guess was as good as mine, because I didn't have a clue what it meant. I just knew I couldn't shake my despair, and I cried with deep emptiness. I now understand that the dream was prophetic, for within a few months, Hugh would be lost in a car accident and our church would be in the midst of a turbulent division in its membership. At the time of the dream, both of these occurrences seemed impossible.

Memories

February 26, 1987 I will never forget Hugh's fiftieth and last birthday. Of course we had a party, and he decided to invite a group of old friends to our home for dinner. What Hugh didn't know was that it was a 'roast' for him. Nor did he expect to see his mother and sister from out of state.

It was a festive affair, with the house full of flowers, balloons, presents, laughter and the pungent fragrance of lasagna in the oven. Our son Bo, who is a chef, prepared an antipasto tray just for the occasion. Hugh was so pleased because it was not only delicious, but gorgeous to look at. Dad was proud to show off the skills of his son. He was also showing off his first grandchild, Austin. Austin's mom and dad, Dee and Kevin, were happily married and expecting their second child, Bryce. David, our youngest, was following in the engineering footsteps of his father, and I, after twenty-nine years of marriage, was turning into a pretty good sidekick. Fifty was a good age to enjoy the fruits of his labor, and this was a man who truly appreciated his family. What more could a man want? The smile on his face said it all!

After dinner, we gathered in the family room and sat Hugh in a place of honor. I had had all of our home movies made into a video, and it was delightful to see the response of the group. *Déjà vu* to say the least! Then all of the guests told their favorite stories about Hugh. His mother, brother and sisters brought old pictures, poems and more stories about growing up with 'big brother.' This was an evening of laughter and tears; a mingling of the young and old; a oneness of heart. It was one of those rare times that was absolutely magical and, oh, how he loved it. In the end, no one wanted to leave. We were celebrating the glory of Hugh's mid-life. Eighteen days later, we would celebrate the glory of his eternal life.

Each of these nine events prepared me in different ways for the road ahead. Without them, I would have been overwhelmed by the sudden and tragic change in my life. *In retrospect, I can now see that God's sustaining grace began long before I needed it, preparing a ground which I did not know would soon be so shaky.*

4
'I WILL BREAK YOU, BUT I WILL USE YOU!'

GEORGE

On November 5, 1964, 'Landslide' Lyndon Johnson was elected president of the United States.[1] As a Texan, I should have found cause for much festivity in my university dormitory, but that night was full of contradictory feelings. Two days prior, my newly-born-again girlfriend had given me a copy of *Living Letters*. This precursor to the *Living Bible* began with Paul's letter to the Romans and was my first exposure to the New Testament. A few hours past midnight, not able to sleep, I settled down once again to read. In a matter of minutes, I was overwhelmed by Romans 6:23 and, kneeling on the floor, asked God for his 'free gift.' This revelation of a new life was instantaneous. I knew that I had been transformed, that God had his hand on my life, and that I must follow his direction at any cost. By morning light, I was packing my car, leaving the university, and heading home to my family in Dallas. I knew I had changed and that I could not stay in my present environment without losing what was now so dear.

Shortly after my conversion, I enrolled in Dallas Bible College where I took one semester of training. The semester proved a blessing as I was given a doctrinal foundation for my faith. In the fall of 1965, I returned to my former university and with the help of several friends, launched a chapter of Inter-Varsity Christian Fellowship. Three years later, I married my IVCF staff worker and former Bible

School classmate, Bonnie Burns, and the two of us were sent to Houston to pioneer new work for IVCF.

Vancouver, here we come!

In 1971, Bonnie and I left Houston for Vancouver, British Columbia to enroll in a new graduate school called Regent College. Its faculty came mostly from the ranks of the Plymouth Brethren, an ecclesiastical tradition which I eventually joined. This movement had strong cessationist roots which ran back to the dispensational godfather John Nelson Darby. Later, Regent added faculty from various traditions, dispelling any anti-charismatic tendencies.

Shortly after my arrival in Vancouver, I was asked to speak on the campus of the University of British Columbia to the local IVCF group. In the rear of the auditorium sat an elderly man. Bob Birch had been the first IVCF worker in Canada, being present when the name Inter-Varsity Christian Fellowship was chosen for the Canadian student work in 1929. Bob watched my ministry with the students and invited me to speak the following Sunday evening at the lively work he pastored, St Margaret's Church.

Feeling greatly honored by his invitation, I was aghast to discover that the church was 'charismatic.' At that time, my theology and experience made me a fire-breathing anti-pentecostal and anti-charismatic, and I could not imagine speaking in such a context. But I went along to the meeting and quickly found myself moved by the worship and the friendliness with which I was received. From that point on, I had many times with Bob and never in our conversations did he ever once ask if I was baptized in the Holy Spirit or if I spoke in tongues. I remember saying to myself, 'If he is a charismatic, he is the most unusual one I have ever met.'

Several months later, Bob invited me to a small luncheon with an Englishman named David Watson. I thought to myself, 'Here comes the heavy! I'm sure this guy is really going to lay on the charismatic trip!' When David stood up to speak, he seemed like a reproduction of another famous English preacher, John R. W. Stott. He sounded like Stott, he expounded the scriptures like Stott, he even held his thumbs in his britches like Stott. This completely confused my program as to what 'charismatics' believed and how they were to act. Leaving the meeting, I said to myself, 'I want to write to that man and find out what makes him tick.'

Evangelical agnostic

My writing to David was delayed, although I knew his address by heart, as I found myself immersed in congregational concerns at Marineview Chapel where I had become a teaching elder. One area was particularly stressful, and I devoted the best part of a year praying for the resolution of that problem. The showdown came, and it seemed obvious to me that God had not heard a word I prayed. So, by an act of my will, I chose to become an evangelical agnostic. I preached like a theist, but in real life I lived like a deist. I believed in the gospel, but I no longer believed that God was actively present or heard my prayers.

I persisted in this state for several months. It was interrupted on a flight out of Los Angeles back to Vancouver after a summer holiday. Faye, who at this point was nine months old, was suffering from an ear infection which caused her to scream in pain once the plane became airborne. In desperation I cried out, 'God, I know you are not listening to my prayers, but if you will just put this child to sleep, I'll start believing and talking to you again.' In a matter of minutes, Faye was out like a light. I found this somewhat disturbing.

Help, there's a charismatic in my bedroom

When I returned from my holiday, I discovered that 'charismatic' influence had been deposited in our church while I was away. Three things happened at this point that were decidedly crucial. First, while eating lunch in the faculty lounge of the University, someone pointed out a new professor and said to me, 'Bob McLeod is from David Watson's church in York.' Knowing that I had failed to write to David and thinking this new man Bob might be able to help, I made friends with him and his wife Marilyn. In a short time, God led them to our congregation and they began to model for us a sober yet powerful relationship with the Holy Spirit.

The second encouragement came from Bonnie. As a good evangelical, she had sublimated many of her mystical desires in the readings of C. S. Lewis and J. R. R. Tolkien. Yet none of these were able to meet the fullest need of her heart. One day, while she was praying for me, God suddenly released within her the very presence of his Spirit. There came a new freshness and vigor to her life, and she spoke in a language she did not know. You can imagine my reaction, as a good 'Brethren worker' who did not really believe these things were possible, when she told me what had happened. Suddenly, our bedroom became a battlefield. Painfully, we tried to reconcile what we had been taught with what was presently happening. I had known Bonnie since our days in Bible College. She mentored me in my walk as a young Christian, and God was using her now to pave a new direction for us. She was the greatest single influence in my discipleship. When we eventually came into agreement about the work of the Spirit, we both saw how every renewal in the Holy Spirit produces fear in others, no matter how gently it is handled.

The third crucial event was a question posed to me by Mark, one of my elders. I was teaching from Romans 5–8 when he approached me and said, 'George, you keep telling us what you don't believe about the Spirit. Why don't you tell us what you do believe'? He nailed me, and I knew it. The only teaching I knew on the Holy Spirit was essentially negative; and I was at a loss to say anything positive.

This question, together with Bonnie's experience, put

me on a one-year search. Every day, I prayed that God would teach me about the Holy Spirit. I also began to read everything I could find on the subject, ranging from classic works to newer testimonies. I spent many days in prayer asking God to fill me with his Spirit. For most of the year, there were no obvious answers. And then, a few little things began to happen. I began having dreams and visions. God even used some of these in the conversion of other people. Something significant was happening.

86 East Parade, York

When we had been with our congregation for three years, we were given a six-week sabbatical. I thought it was about time that I finally talked with David Watson. Our marriage had suffered enough strain in this search for the Spirit, and it was time to resolve some of my own questions.

After arriving in York, we had our first scheduled appointment with David. Sitting in his living room, Bonnie and I poured out stories highlighting the past five years. His comments at the end were the most assuring words I ever heard: 'Congratulations, you have both been filled with the Holy Spirit!' Bonnie needed to hear from this reputable authority that even though my experience had been different from hers; mine was slow and spread out over a year, while hers was sudden and sensationally transforming – both of us had been filled with the same Holy Spirit. With this assurance under our belts, we spent the remaining time absorbing the spiritual life at David's church, St Michael's le Belfrey. There was worship, dance and drama. There were prophecies and evangelistic outreach. There was so much more than I ever believed possible for the church.

Returning to Vancouver, we began to learn as much as we could about the gifts of the Holy Spirit. We began to exercise words of knowledge and prophecy as we prayed for people. Within a year, all alone in my study, I began speaking in tongues. It was such an unusual thing for me that I did not realize for several days what had happened. It just seemed like the right thing at the right time to assist me in prayer. At the same time, Marineview chapel was growing in numbers and in its understanding of renewal.[2]

Those controversial gifts

Though still not in the mainstream of the charismatic movement, Bonnie and I continued to practice and teach what God had been doing in our own lives. One Christmas morning, in 1981, I was awakened about 4:00 a.m. I knew at that moment I was to write a book for evangelicals, like myself, who did not believe in the present gifting of the Holy Spirit. God impressed on my heart that large numbers of evangelicals were going to be awakened by the Spirit and would begin to exercise the gifts of the Spirit. This leading was so strong that I was given by the Spirit full chapter titles, outlines and even specific dictations of particular paragraphs. Within a few days, the project had begun.

In the spring of 1983, *Those Controversial Gifts* was released by Inter-Varsity Press.[3] Two weeks later, I was stricken with a mysterious illness that caused me to be bed-ridden for three months and it took another year for me to fully recover. I now know that a major spiritual attack was launched against us at that time as the devil resisted the notion of evangelicals being released in the Spirit. I found it humorous that when the doctors gave a tentative name to my sickness, 'Bornholm's Disease,' and I looked it up in a medical dictionary, the 'Devil's Grip' was listed as its nickname.

In July of 1983, I joined the pastoral team of Burnaby Christian Fellowship. That same summer, the World Council of Churches held its Sixth Assembly in Vancouver. During the Assembly, a number of congregations in Vancouver sponsored three evenings of special speakers giving our response to the WCC agenda. John Wimber was one of three invited guests.

I had never met John before, but David Watson had

once raved about him and the church he pastored in Anaheim. I met him in his hotel for dinner and, since I was still suffering from my sickness, John invited me up to his room to receive prayer. 'I sense you have a spirit of rejection. Has anyone ever shown major rejection towards you?' was his opening question. I mumbled some comment and John continued to pray. Over the next two years, the truthfulness of John's discernment became apparent.

On two separate occasions, unknown to anyone but Bonnie and myself, God graphically and quickly, within about thirty minutes, healed me of a childhood rejection experience. The effects have been dramatic and freed me for pastoral ministry in a way I never knew before.

Cancer strikes

August, 1983 John was not gone more than a few weeks when doctors discovered a malignant tumor connected to Bonnie's fallopian tube. Although they wanted to operate immediately, it was a few days before we could secure a hospital bed for her. During those days, God came close to my wife and assured her of healing. Surgery removed the tumor, a rare ugly mass of which only twenty-five had been seen in the last forty years at the Vancouver Cancer Clinic. Amazingly the doctors said they had gotten all the cancer and that just a few bouts of radiation were necessary.

When we returned to the hospital two weeks later, the doctor's assessment changed dramatically. Now they were suggesting a full year of chemotherapy and radiation to ensure that the cancer would not return. We traveled to the Princess Margaret Hospital in Toronto, one of the finest cancer clinics in North America, to get a second opinion. The Director of the Ontario Cancer Institute supervised the case and concluded that the danger of the return of cancer was far more serious than the Vancouver doctors had suggested. Essentially, no one thought she would live more than a year without immediate post-surgical treatment.

With this hard news churning in our stomachs, we took a ride to Niagara Falls. For a good part of the day we stood before the rushing falls, the spray in our faces indistinguishable from our tears. That night, we returned to a medical friend's home and hammered out our options. As the conversation went back and forth, I could tell that Bonnie was growing in faith and that she was about to enter this journey without any medical help whatsoever.

Returning to Vancouver, we tried to begin a normal life once again, in spite of the sentence of death hanging over our heads. Two things were particularly helpful to me during this season. The first was a sense of answered prayer. In desperation, and still in much physical weakness, I cried out to God one evening, 'Lord, just let her live until these kids all get in [primary] school!' It was a brief petition, but I had an overwhelming sense that it was a prayer which had been duly noted by God and would be answered.

I also had a vivid dream where in a medical lecture hall, I was approached by a doctor who happened in real life to be one of my elders. Very confidently he said to me, 'George, we have examined Bonnie's case, and we can assure you that she will be O.K.' When I awoke the next morning, the dream was at the forefront of my conscious mind. I added this to the sense of answered prayer and concluded that I could be at peace since the matter was clearly in the hands of God. For almost five years, without any medical treatment, Bonnie was perfectly healthy.

'No place but Texas'

March 20, 1987 Canadians who live on the rainy West Coast are always skimming ways to get sunshine. Bonnie and I, along with several of our church staff, decided to have a holiday in Hawaii. But as good as the weather was, something began to eat at me while I was away. Since I had lived in Vancouver for sixteen years, raising my children there and even becoming a citizen, I assumed I would live there the rest of my life. I had already picked out the place for our retirement. But now, with the relaxation of sand and surf, I began to have the gut feeling that God was calling me back to Texas.

Unbeknownst to me, in that same week, Carolyn lost Hugh and was wrestling not only with her loneliness, but with major decisions about her future.

May 18, 1987 Arriving home from the trip, I began to see reasons why God might be asking me to return to Texas. Pre-eminent in my thinking was the care for my aging parents in Dallas. In my mind I concluded, 'If I can be four or five driving hours away, then I can get to them if they should need any help.' On this particular morning, I awoke, my feet barely on the floor, when the Lord spoke specifically to me, 'You're going to Arlington, Texas and the Deere's will join you!' It was such a loud voice in my head, I could not have missed it if I wanted to. Over the next twenty-four hours, several friends and relatives called and gave independent confirmation that Arlington was indeed the place I should move. As to the 'Deere's,' I assumed this meant Jack Deere who was a professor at Dallas Theological Seminary and had become interested in the work of the Holy Spirit through a visit with Dr John White.[4] Jack and Leesa did indeed join us for the first year as we planted Grace Vineyard Christian Fellowship.

Again, unknown to me, widow Carolyn Driggers lived in Arlington, Texas.

I began to make plans for the move. I resigned from Burnaby Christian Fellowship and made a trip to Arlington to scout the lay of the land. The move would entail the planting of a new church, and I was unsure of the community's receptivity for the things I had to offer. To my great surprise, a group of Christians had been meeting for several years and praying for a new church. Within twenty-four hours of my arrival in Arlington, I had made contact with this group and the leaders expressed great excitement about our coming. With this nucleus, we started the Vineyard in September of 1987.

Before I left Vancouver, the Lord spoke to me several times, repeating the same words, 'I will break you, but I will use you.' Two sides of me greeted this word, 'Lord, I'm sure I need some breaking, but go easy on me!' *Little did I know, that the next five years would be the hardest of my adult life.*

One more time

May 7, 1988 We had a successful start to the Vineyard, and I was having a great time doing the things I like best. This all came to a halt when Bonnie's cancer reappeared. In my diary I wrote, 'We now know that Bonnie has a tumor [second] growing in her abdomen. The doctors assume that it is a reoccurrence of the cancer [1983] and it looks most severe. One doctor said that this tumor would be like "concrete spread in grass" rather than "an apple hanging from a branch."'

Surgery was immediately necessary and was followed by a trip to Athens, Greece for a treatment which was an alternative method to chemotherapy. Bonnie enjoyed her time away, especially as she and Donna Bromley were able to spend a week in Israel. However, all attempts to halt the reoccurrence of tumors were unsuccessful. As a result, we faced the same ordeal in April and December of 1989. When the fifth tumor appeared in December of 1990, Bonnie and I concluded that we would do nothing more on the medical front, choosing instead to trust God for everything we needed. Owing to the fact that no insurance company would provide us coverage, thousands of dollars were given to us by friends, relatives and the church, to care for her needs. We now felt we could no longer impose on such graciousness. Besides, Bonnie had had her fill of hospitals and bed-bound days in recovery; she was ready to walk to the end of the road and find out what was going to happen. When I learned of Bonnie's second tumor in May of 1988, I began what one friend called 'anticipatory grieving.' I knew I was about to lose my wife and nothing I could do would change that fact.

For years, I successfully avoided any major tragedy in my life. Little traumas were easily sedated by diligence and a dose of sensitive prayer. Smugly, I assumed I could outwit any disruption thrown at me. At the same time, I believed I was one of God's 'good guys,' and as long as I persisted in faith, surely he would navigate my little boat around troubled waters. I knew there would be some minor trials along the way, a little sickness here or minor financial pressures there, but I thought to myself, 'Surely, he will not devastate my life, if I remain faithful!' But when Bonnie's cancer returned, I was stunned. I sat for hours staring out the window, changing my glance only to look at the wall. Tears constantly filled my eyes, but no sounds were uttered other than guttural moans. The days turned into weeks, then months. Sometimes I would muster courage and relate to people with some degree of intelligence and kindness. Years before, when Pope John Paul I died, my pre-school son Scott sat watching the evening news with teary eyes. Looking up at me he said, 'The hope [not the Pope] is dead.' So with me, my hope was dead.

The pain was compounded when I had to relate the details to my children. Without hesitation, they asked for an explanation of the circumstances. The words I could muster for the moment, the ones I had chewed and digested for many years, I offered to them. But for them, as it was for me, it was a sparse meal.

Over the years, I watched numerous families manage their personal tragedies: deformed babies, teen suicide, car wrecks, cancer, and even murder. Some seemed to grow through the crisis, while others wilted like plants without water. I wondered which I would be? Would I betray the values I had taught for years? Had I deceived myself in answering the real questions of life? Would I tough it out, no matter what I believed? I thought I would make it since my emotional genes were fairly firm, but I did not know how.

Long before my crisis emerged, I thought I understood one principle – if you do not have an answer to the question of personal suffering *before* the event transpires, you are not likely to get an answer in the *midst* of the crisis. You may get your answer, if one does exist, sometime *after* the event, but expecting it *during* the crisis is asking too much. So, armed with this knowledge I prepared myself, if tragedy should strike.

May 23, 1988 On this day, confused and discouraged, I wrote in my diary, 'We are battling for Bonnie's life.' On that very same day, only three miles south of my home, God was speaking to a widow I had never met. The five lines he spoke to her on that day would eventually sooth my broken heart and bring me incredible joy. It would be over three and one-half years before I got to hear those words, but when I finally heard them, I understood that: *Although God seems absent in crisis, he has already orchestrated his plans for blessing.*

5
CRISIS IN CIRCUMSTANCES

CAROLYN

March 24, 1987 A week after the memorial service, a meeting was arranged for the company-benefits people to see me and explain my future. I hadn't thought much about my economic future, because I knew everything was well taken care of by Hugh. However, the financial picture was quite different from what I expected. To begin with, Hugh was fifty years old at the time of the accident and his early retirement benefits were not due to start until his fifty-fifth birthday. On top of this, the company was in reorganizational bankruptcy which greatly changed the value of the stock plan and other benefits. Hugh was also on vacation when the accident occurred. The bottom line was simple; there would be no income for five years, other than insurance and limited benefits. We were all in shock! I stood in my living room that night with Hugh's brother and my son-in-law, clasping our hands in prayer. We were devastated at this unexpected turn of events. None of us could believe what we had just heard, nor could we attempt to conceive what was ahead.

That night I told the Lord, 'This is not what I expected.' He said to me, 'Carolyn, there were eleven disciples at the foot of the cross and it wasn't what they expected either, but look at what I did later.'

Connectors

March 25, 1987 I have certain friends whom I call 'connectors.' Their gifts lie in the realm of connecting people with needs to people who can help. The day after I learned of my financial situation, I called Pat Godfrey, one of my dearest connectors, who had offered her assistance. I asked her, 'Can you come?' and she replied, 'I'm on my way.' During the day, we looked at my liabilities, my assets and options. Immediately, we realized I had to do something quick. I needed to make an investment that would provide an income. I smiled as I realized that I had been taken care of all my life; in fact, my son-in-law called me 'Scarlet.' In short, making a major financial decision had never been mine to make alone. After much counsel and prayer, I took my little lump of money and invested it in a dry-cleaning business.

As with 'Miss Scarlet,' I didn't know much about the business world, but this was God's way of moving me to a higher place of faith. Faith does not come until we step out on what is unseen. It is believing God will do what he has told us he will do. Needless to say, this was really a big step. The Texas economy was slow at that time and it was in the middle of summer, when the cleaning business is at its lowest ebb. Added to this was my inexperience in running a business. But I felt God was giving me a new perspective, and I was committed to trusting him, although I had to ignore a lot of negative comments from people who were not privy to God's leading for me. Naturally, they were afraid for me.

The plan was for me to invest in my children. I would buy the cleaners and pay for it. Then I could lease the business to my son-in-law, Kevin. It would be my income and his career. When I made this proposition to Kevin, he didn't give me an answer immediately because it would be a big step for him. His university degree was in marketing finance and he had been with a very large company for several years. Kevin and Dee were expecting their second child and he had to think of their security. Well, as God would have it, I had to come face to face with the reality that I had to make the decision to do this *alone*. I agonized over the thought of going into business

Crisis in Circumstances

for myself, in a job that would be very demanding with very long hours. But I realized that God had called me to this place, and I had a sole responsibility to make a decision. I decided the cleaners was my best option.

Very early the next morning, Bo found me in the family room and asked me if I had thought about what I would do if Kevin decided not to run the cleaners. 'Yes,' I said, 'I have. In fact, last night I realized I had to make that decision. I decided to go on with the cleaners, even if it means doing it alone.' He then made a very generous offer. He said, 'Mom, I will give you a year of my life. I will stay with you until you learn the business and you are comfortable with it.'

The children were remarkably supportive during this time. I was so grateful that they were there for me and that God was doing such a big work in their lives as well. Kevin called shortly and said that he would go into business with me, but he went to my two sons to be sure he was not infringing on their positions or ambitions. Since their careers were established in different directions, they were very pleased with his decision.

Kevin planned to give notice to leave his job on the last day of July; this would give him a month to prepare for the training and opening of the cleaners in September. Then one Friday afternoon he called and said, 'They just announced the closing of our division and they are laying everyone off on the first of July, with six weeks severance pay.' I could tell he was overwhelmed by the news. He then continued, 'You know, I've really been vacillating back and forth as to whether or not I was doing the right thing. It's like God is saying, "Is this enough confirmation for you?"'

As if that were not enough, the store was moving to completion much faster than the owners of the franchise expected. We would be opening six weeks early, which is very unusual. This meant that we would open July 1st. Kevin asked his boss if he would lay him off the first of June since he needed a month to train.

No problem there! All of the timetables came together perfectly.

Learning the ropes

April – June, 1987 For the next three months, Kevin and I learned all the 'in's' and 'out's' of the dry-cleaning business. I always wondered how the cleaners could take my pile of dirty clothes and get them back clean, and to the right person. Now, I knew!

Kevin jumped right in with unlimited energy and quickly picked up on the system. He was smart and aggressive with a hands-on attitude, while I was overwhelmed with the magnitude of the job. Frankly, my body was exhausted. I couldn't remember feeling so weary. Yet, my spirit was joyful and exhilarated. I found myself going to bed late and rising early every day, fully refreshed. I felt caught up in a moving force, and I knew I could trust where it was taking me.

Feed my sheep

June 5, 1987 After a long day at work, Elliott Johnson, my pastor, called. He was preparing a series of sermons entitled, 'Under the Cross.' He wanted to have three people from our congregation share before each sermon what God was doing in their lives. He asked me if I would be the first.

I felt his request was impossible. I was afraid of speaking to large crowds, and I had no idea what I would say. But Elliott encouraged me to pray about it and give him my answer the next day. I put poor, pitiful me to bed and talked to my sister in California. Her parting words were, 'This is too much to ask of you right now.' I agreed!

As a child, I was raised in the church, I had an intellectual understanding of Jesus Christ, and I lived by a moral Christian code. But God and Jesus were always up in heaven, while I was running my life down on earth. I could always remember having an empty hole inside of me that nothing seemed to fill. In fact, every major

Crisis in Circumstances

accomplishment that should have filled me with satisfaction fell through the hole and left me emptier than before. As the years passed, I was blessed with everything Cinderella would have hoped for in her fairytale life: a wonderful childhood, marrying my college sweetheart, three beautiful children, the home of my dreams, the right clothes to wear, the right places to go, and the right people to be with. The dream life of every woman, and yet, the empty hole within me swallowed it all up.

In my mid-thirties, I began to question, 'Is this all there is?' I was pressed to search for an answer as I suffered with a friend through a life and death crisis. Out of the ordeal, I consented to attend a 'Life In The Spirit' seminar with my friend. The classes met every Friday night for six weeks. After the final meeting, I came home with a respiratory infection. My chest felt like I had a truck parked on it. I retreated to my bed, lying on my back with my hands crossed on my chest. As I began to reflect upon the evening, I decided to put God to the test. I cried out in the darkness, 'I am seeking you. I am asking you to reveal yourself to me. I am knocking on your door. If you will remove this pain from my chest, I will give my life to you.' In an instant I felt my hands float up from my chest and the pain was gone. I took a deep breath and a big smile consumed my face. He was there! In the next second, I was aware of God's presence in the room and in my life. He had filled my empty hole. I realized then that nothing could fill that hole but Jesus, for it was shaped like him.

I had been a believer for about ten years when Elliott asked me to speak, but I was still scared. The day after our conversation June 6th, I awakened to a glorious morning. I went into the kitchen for my morning coffee, before starting my prayer time. I settled myself for the daily devotional and opened my Bible to John 21:16. 'Do you truly love me? . . . Feed my sheep.' I laughed. He had done it to me again; he had answered the question before I had time to ask.

A few days later, as I was thinking about what to say

to the church, I began to cry. I knew God wanted me to do this, but I had no strength. In my weakness, the Lord spoke and said, 'Why are you afraid? These are my children, your brothers and sisters. Speak to them for me. All you have to do is be willing to stand before them and I will give you the words.' A deep peace came over me and the fear was gone. This would be no different to coming down that mountain on skis. Perfect love casts out fear!

The Sunday I spoke, I stood before a full house with no notes, a small Bible and a large handkerchief. When I turned and looked at those people, I was filled with calm and God's love. I opened my mouth and the words began to flow. The anointing of God upon your words is a powerful experience and one I will never forget. I couldn't remember what I said, but I got the tape and felt blessed by the message.

Overnight success!

July 1, 1987 This was the big day, the grand opening of our cleaners. Three days later, our store was packed to overflowing with clothes. By July 10th, our cleaners was, in businesss terms, an overnight success. Our biggest need was more help; this gave the children an opportunity to get involved and learn about their investment. *Eight days after our opening, God had already established my income.* I had been thinking more along the lines of three years, but the racks were full, the numbers were right, and we had hired all the help we needed. This was our agreement, Kevin had his career and I had an income. (After the store had been open for nearly a year, I was speechless when I heard from my accountant that my personal income from the cleaning business would be about the same figure my husband made after thirty years in his career.)

In retrospect, I do not know why God chose to bless me in such a gracious fashion. I have seen plenty of widows and single parents who have difficulty making an income, so I know this to be the provision of God. At the same time, I believe that obedience releases the blessings of God. If we walk in his ways and follow his direction, we can be assured that he will bless our every step.

Write the book

July 12, 1987   July turned out to be a month of wonder-working miracles. I had opened my own cleaners. I had spoken to my home church about the provision of God and his sustaining grace and God's care for me continued, this time through Hugh's grandmother. From her estate, I was given the exact downpayment I needed to purchase a new car. All of my needs were being looked after.

Since I was now not needed at the cleaners, I began to wonder what I would do with myself. During my devotions, the Lord spoke to me again. 'I want you to write a book about everything that has happened. It will be written and published.' I sat in disbelief and said, 'How could this be? I don't write! I don't even write postcards to my mother!' Then he said, 'Call Carolyn Boyd.' That was something else I was not in the habit of doing – calling people early, particularly on Sunday mornings. But then I thought, 'Well, maybe she is going to write this book!'

In obedience, I picked up the phone and made the call to Carolyn. We shared some nice pleasantries, and then she said, 'I'm tired of just being busy, I want God to call me to something.' To that I replied, 'I think he just did. He told me to call you about this book.' When I told her the details, she responded with an enthusiastic yes!

We got together later that week and listened to the tape of the talk I had given at church. She was encouraged that there was more than sufficient material for a book, but then she added, 'No one but you can write this book. You lived it! It's your story to tell.' Well, I thought, if I write a book, it will be a miracle that will rival the parting of the Red Sea.

I soon found Carolyn to be a great organizer and visionary. She had a vision for the ministry of the book and, because she was a connector, things began to work. In August, we spent a week away and finished the first draft. The book was rough, a mere bag of bones, but we knew in God's timing these 'dry bones' would soon be connected and come to life. Little did I realize that in five years' time, God would grant me a husband who was an experienced writer and that my story would become our story together.

'They will not ring your doorbell'

January 16, 1992 After a year of grieving Hugh's death and opening a business, although I was not particularly lonely, friends with good intentions began encouraging me to start dating. I had some thoughts that I might marry again, but the more I entered the world of single men, the more I resisted the idea. Hugh was not a perfect husband, but compared to the options before me, no one could be his match. What I found most common in the men I dated was a combination of unprocessed pain, an absolute phobia about marital commitment, and a weak understanding of following Jesus Christ as Lord. They were 'churched,' but that was all.

One man was particularly enjoyable, but I knew that we had no future. This January day, I broke off the relationship and announced to my friends that I had had it with dating in 'shark-infested waters.' From that day on, I was retiring to paint and write. Naturally, they tried to talk me out of my decision. 'Carolyn, the right man will not just walk up and ring your doorbell!'

Two weeks later, George did just that!

6
'O LORD ... GIVE ME SUCCESS'

GEORGE

In the last months of her life, Bonnie performed several heroic deeds. Like all terminally ill people, she endured her share of pain and the humiliation that comes when a body wears out. But she went beyond the call of duty on several occasions: saying goodbye to Faye before she left for Scotland, giving Scott a pep talk, and holding Meredyth in her arms nightly before bedtime. Just after I arrived home from Scotland, Bonnie called Donna into the bedroom and gave her all her nice clothing. One by one, Donna modeled each item, getting Bonnie's helpful hints on just the right scarf and jewelry for each outfit. I sat on the bed, stunned by what was happening. It was inspirational and surreal at the same time. I thought to myself, all the tears ever shed in movies like 'Beaches,' 'Love Story,' and 'A Field of Dreams,' could not express the scene I had just witnessed. Two best friends, planning a future in which only one would participate.

One additional evening stands out in my mind. Often I would go into her bedroom and lay my head in her lap, crying softly. Stroking my hair, she would comfort me and encourage me to carry on. She was very specific about the details of her funeral and made sure I would bury her in a 'pine box.' We talked. We cried. We planned life without her. On this particular evening, she gave me some specific instructions about a new wife. For years she had encouraged me to marry again if she ever died. She did not want to leave, but she wanted to make sure I was cared for in any eventuality. As with all couples in conversation, you can tell much about the tone of voice and the names used. In our family, there was a world of difference between 'Honey,' 'George!,' and 'George Haydon!' That night she had the 'George Haydon' look on her face as we began to talk. 'I want you to marry a Texas woman. I want you to fall desperately in love with her. And make sure she loves Meredyth just like Margaret Saunders did in England.' Margaret and Teddy Saunders were particularly comforting to Meredyth when we took Faye to the United Kingdom in October.

As in the evening with Donna, I was stunned. Bonnie was not only permitting remarriage, she was prophesying my new partner. We both knew that one of the essentials in our marriage had been our covenant, a relational loyalty that could not be severed. In fact, the motto of my Irish ancestry had been 'fidelis ad urnam,' or 'faithful unto death.' Now she was permitting me to end the covenant and begin again. As you do in those moments when the living are still present, I quickly changed the subject to her needs. However, weeks after her death, these words would return as comfort and direction.

Terry Law

In the summer of 1990, Bonnie and I attended a conference in Kansas City. The first evening I was there, I noticed a man sitting several rows in front of me. He did not know me, but I knew of him. His name was Terry Law and he had been associated over the years with Oral Roberts University. His story had been told to me by several friends and later I read his own account in *Yet Will I Praise Him*.[1] Terry's wife was killed in a car wreck while he was in Europe doing evangelistic ministry. Shirley, the woman he then eventually married, was also a widow, losing her husband to a brain tumor. Although they had never met, both were raising their children as single parents and living in Tulsa, Oklahoma. One Saturday morning, Terry dressed his kids and took them to McDonald's for breakfast. Shirley and her kids were not dressed yet, but they already had a hot breakfast waiting in the kitchen. At that point, Shirley heard the Lord say, 'Get dressed and go to McDonald's for breakfast!' She thought it a strange request and resisted for a few moments. But the impression grew stronger, so she followed the Lord's prompting and took the kids to McDonald's. Having seen Terry in her home church years before, and having friends who had served on his team, she was familiar with his face when she saw him in the restaurant. As you can guess, they met and eventually married.

When I saw Terry sitting with Shirley, I prayed this prayer, 'Lord, if I ever lose Bonnie, I pray you will grant me a wife as *supernaturally* as you have done for Terry Law.' Eighteen months later, that request was granted.

Two weeks off

There is no rule book for mourning, so everyone needs to do what they consider honoring to both the dead and the living. As a pastor, I was aware that I could not do my job effectively as a single man. Others have no difficulty in doing this, but celibacy is not one of my gifts. In my own mind, I concluded that I needed to wait at least three months (twelve weeks), before I could pursue any dating relationship.

During this waiting season, I not only dealt with the last residue of my grieving, something which I had done intently for two years already, but I also repeated the prayer of Abraham's servant when he went in search of a wife for Isaac: 'O Lord . . . give me success today' (Gen 24:12). I knew I could not date like other singles; my only hope was that God would hear my prayer and sovereignly grant me a wife.

January 20, 1992 On this day, I got out of bed and walked into the bathroom to shave. Before I reached the lavatory, I heard in my head these words, '**April 11th**.' They were so loud they resonated through my head. Of course, I did not have a clue what it meant, but I knew something would happen on that day, or at least the day would be special for someone.

January 28, 1992 Several days before this date, I saw my friend Pennye Wilemon at a basketball game and told her humorously that I was paying a 'finder's fee' for a good wife. She promised to think about it. At 5:30 that morning, according to her own testimony, Pennye was strangely awakened. Not able to sleep, she asked the Lord who she could suggest for me to take out. Immediately the name Carolyn Driggers came to mind. The Wilemons and the Driggers were former acquaintances and saw one another occasionally at church. Pennye called that evening to tell me what had happened, relaying the following information: 'She is about four years older than you, with three grown children and two grandchildren. But George, she is "*well-preserved*".' I told her that any recommendation she might have would surely suit me, since I trusted her taste in women, and told her to find out what she could and call me back.

That evening as I was praying and reminding the Lord that *he* was the one who wrote the words, 'It is not good for man to be alone' (Gen 2:18), he replied, 'I have taken one week off.' This made little sense, but it was aptly noted. As I prayed the next evening, the Lord said to me again, 'I have now taken two weeks off.' 'Two weeks off of what?' I asked myself.

January 30, 1992 It's really beginning to sound like a soap opera, isn't it? Well, Pennye called back to say that Carolyn would be glad to go out if I should ask. I wasted no time and within a few minutes, we were set for the next night to go to Scott's basketball game.

January 31, 1992 As I said before, I had imposed upon myself a three-month (twelve-week) waiting period. Here I was about to take Carolyn out only ten weeks after Bonnie's death. It then dawned on me that this was the Lord's meaning when he said, 'I have taken two weeks off.'

Several weeks later, I realized that seventy days (ten

weeks) was the time of Egyptian mourning for the death of Joseph's father (Gen 50:3). It was at the same time that Carolyn and I determined that 'April 11th' was indeed to be our wedding date. I then saw that from the first date I had with Carolyn until we were married, it was also seventy days (ten weeks). I had been given seventy days to mourn and seventy days to prepare for a new marriage.

7
MORE THAN A LOVE STORY

CAROLYN AND GEORGE

January 31, 1992 *(George)* I was nervous as I left for my first date with Carolyn. After all, it was something I had not done in over twenty-five years. Carolyn later informed me, being herself wise to the single world, that you never go on a blind date for more than a few hours, in case you cannot stand the person you are with. Well, like it or not, we were set for a seven-hour date, by the time we drove to Scott's out-of-town basketball game, had dinner and returned home.

As we drove to the game, I was so nervous I found it hard to look Carolyn in the face, so I left my sunglasses on as long as I could. She, however, was easy and gracious, making me feel I was doing just fine. By the time we arrived at the game, an unusual attraction began to emerge. I liked her red hair, the way she dressed, her humor, and her gentleness. The gym was smelly and dirty, but she appeared to be perfectly comfortable with our first outing.

After the game, we drove back to Fort Worth for dinner. Two things happened that were rather strange. First, somewhere in the middle of our conversation our vocabulary began to change. We starting using first person plurals (e.g. 'we,' 'our') rather than first person singulars (e.g. 'I'). This was somewhat shocking to both of us. Then later, after I had pontificated to her about the certainty of God speaking today, Carolyn said, 'I have something to tell you, but I can't do it until I know you better.' I thought it interesting, but I was not all that curious.

We returned to her house, had a little coffee, and talked some more. During this time, I learned about her life with Hugh and the manuscript she had produced. As I was listening to her, I had a vision. In the middle of her chest was a thermometer, registering 98 degrees. In black letters I saw the word 'obedience.' It seemed to me that the Lord was saying that whatever characteristics Carolyn possessed, I could be assured that she would be obedient to God. As I was leaving, I put my arms gently around her and said, 'I think there is something special about this evening, but I don't know what it is.' I then rushed home to beat Scott's curfew, thinking it quite an embarrassment that I should return later than him from the game.

(*Carolyn*) I could really sympathize with George's apprehensions about our first date. I had been in the single world for four years and had seen 'the good, the bad, and the ugly.' I remembered the anxiety I felt in the first date I had after Hugh's death. I was a nervous wreck. Just as a fickle high-school girl, I could not, for the life of me, determine what I would wear. Like a fashion show model, I emptied my closet dozens of times, ranging in dress from a librarian to a call girl. In the end, I had to phone my daughter Dee to ask her what to wear. So, I knew George would be nervous as he came to pick me up.

During this time, my mind was really focused on my sister in California who was scheduled for major surgery. I was on the phone with her when George called to ask me out. I thought I would see him after I returned, but in the conversation with Jean, we determined that it was best for me to come on Sunday, rather than Friday. I called George back and said I would be happy to go out with him.

Having been widowed, I knew the emotional pain that George was bound to be suffering. I also knew the loneliness and confusion of the single world and hoped that he would not be too shocked by his entrance into this arena. I had just arrived home from a busy day when he pulled up. Catching a glimpse of him as he walked up the side-walk, I said to myself, 'Hum! Cute!'

George loaded me into his van and we headed for the ballgame. Conversation flowed easily as we told one another our stories and the way God had taken care of us. At the restaurant, George asked me a most peculiar question. 'Carolyn, do you like men?' I wondered if it was a trick question, but decided to answer it as honestly as I could. 'Yes, I do and I always have. In fact, I believe most women do like men.' He replied, 'I believe most women hate men because of what they have done to them.' I was surprised. On the way home, George made one more interesting comment. He said, 'Carolyn, I can't believe that you are not married yet!' Frankly, I admitted, 'I'm very picky!'

'Believe me when I speak'

February 1, 1992 *(George)* Poor me, I could not get to sleep until 4:30 a.m. Carolyn had given me a copy of her manuscript and I finished it within a few hours. After that, all I could do was toss and turn and think about the lady I had known for less than twelve hours. Awake again at 7:30 a.m., I swallowed my foolish pride and called her on the phone. Thankfully, she was already awake. 'I have one question; was that regular or decaffinated coffee you served me last night?' When Carolyn assured me it was 'decaf,' I thought to myself, 'I'm in trouble!'

After we talked for a few minutes, Carolyn said, 'I think I need to tell you the word the Lord spoke to me several years ago!' Being the conscientious person I am, I sat up in my bed, grabbed a yellow legal pad and pen, and asked her to tell me what he said. She then told me of several events that arrested her attention. One day, while sitting with golfing friends at lunch, the Lord directed her attention to a man she had never seen before, walking towards her in the clubhouse. The Spirit said to her 'This is your new neighbor.' Within a few minutes, her, friends mentioned the man's name and it was confirmed that he indeed had bought the house next to Carolyn. The following day, the Lord spoke to her again while she was in her backyard. 'I told you what I did yesterday so that you will believe me when I speak, even if you don't understand.'

It was now the third day of hearing God speak specifically, May 23, 1988. As I said previously, I had recorded in my diary that very same day, 'We are now battling for Bonnie's life.' On that day, Carolyn was sweeping her back porch when the Lord said:

'You are going to have a relationship with this man.

It's not who he is, but who he will be.

He will go to the Grace Vineyard.

You will marry.

You will minister together out of the book.'

For over three and one-half years, Carolyn and her friends prayed over this word and tried to make it fit the various successive stages of her life. She thought for a long while that the revelation implied relationships with several men. In all those years, it never dawned on her to go to Grace Vineyard, where I was the pastor, to see if she could find such a person. She did know that ministry from the book probably referred to the manuscript she had written about Hugh's death.

So, here I was, bundled up in bed with my yellow note pad as Carolyn was about to tell me what the Lord had said to her years before. Only a few hours before, I had tutored Carolyn with these words: 'If the Lord speaks, it will be specifically answered. You don't need to bend any word to fit. They will automatically fall into place.' She was now about to make a *believer out of me*. 'Go ahead,

I want to write it down,' I said. Slowly she began to tell me what she had heard.

'You're going to have a relationship with this man.'

'That's good, she is going to meet a man,' I thought.

'It's not who he is, but who he will be.'

I didn't know what that meant. Later, my friend Glenn Terrell would say, 'When she received the word, you were not a widower. Now you are!'

'He will go to the Grace Vineyard.'

'That's interesting. I wonder who the guy might be!'

'You will marry.'

At this point it dawned on me that I *might* be a candidate for this word.

'You will minister together out of the book.'

The night before, when Carolyn told me of the manuscript she had written, I had thought to myself, 'Wouldn't it be interesting if Carolyn and I married and wrote a book on Bonnie and Hugh?'

When she finished telling me these words, I looked at the words I had just written, then took the phone in my hand and held it away from my unbelieving head for a few seconds. Then, forsaking all foolish pride, I shouted:

'I'm the man!'

This absolutely blew Carolyn's 'successive stages theory' into the ozones. She excused herself from the phone and commenced to cry for the rest of the day. She knew, even as naive as it sounded, that I could indeed be the man God had called her to marry.

That evening we went out again, coming home early to meet Meredyth and Scott. It did not take more than a few minutes for the children to take to Carolyn. Even 'Boscoe the Wonder Dog' was giving his approval. I watched carefully as Meredyth got to know Carolyn, because I knew this would be the real test if God was indeed calling us together. The relationship was sweeter than I could have ever imagined.

(*Carolyn*) When George shouted on the phone, 'I'm the man!' I was numb and could not speak. After a few minutes of silence, he said, 'How are you doing?' I responded, 'I'm not doing good at all, and I want to run away from you as fast as I can.' George did his best to console me and said he would call me back later in the afternoon. I spent the rest of the day crying and wrestling with God. Before I met George, I was convinced of one thing, I did not want to marry a doctor or a pastor. Now I had a pastor, with three kids, including teenagers, telling me he was the fulfillment of the word God had given me. Frankly, I was attracted to George, but the rest of the package seemed overwhelming. This was not the picture I had painted for my future, and it was not the life I wanted. Throughout the day I argued with God, alternating between resistance and submission. In the end I lay down on the floor and cried out, 'Lord, if this is what you want me to do, I will do it.' Friends and family who dropped by for a visit thought I had gone off the deep end and were alarmed, but I knew the struggle was necessary. By the time I met George for dinner that night, I sensed I could joyfully embrace the will of God for me.

A week of tears

February 2–11, 1992 (*George*) The following Sunday morning, Carolyn had to go to Orange, California to be with her sister who was having surgery. Before she left, I asked her for a picture and told her to call me as soon as she could. After a few days, we began the ritual of nightly phone calls, advancing the stock of AT&T considerably. It was also a time in which I was overwhelmed with the emotions of love and the goodness of God. For three solid days I cried, stopping only to go to church and eat in public. For me it was the first fruits of the promise I had given my children, 'Just watch, God will show his goodness towards us.'

The scriptures began to flow in my direction, just as if they had me personally in mind when they were written:

> The Lord blessed the latter part of Job's life more than the first (Job 42:12).

> A father to the fatherless, a defender of widows, is God in his holy dwelling. God sets the lonely in families (Ps 68:5–6).
>
> Though you have made me see troubles, many and bitter, you will restore my life again; from the depths of the earth you will again bring me up. You will increase my honor and comfort me once again (Ps 71:20–21).

It was at this time I began to express my feelings for Carolyn more clearly. I composed the following letter, which I gave to her the day I asked her to marry me.

> Two weeks ago today, I did not know you from Adam. One week later, I wired you flowers with the note, 'One week – the rest of our lives.' Some will no doubt chide us with 'love at first sight' epitaphs, but we both know that it is the good hand of God which has brought this about so speedily. So, I have more on my mind today than just asking you to be my Valentine.
>
> But first I want to record for you the thoughts that came to me on February 2–3. I was reviewing my feelings of the two previous days and asking myself the question, 'Am I falling in love with Carolyn Maxine Driggers?' The answer came to me as a series of essays (which I could describe for hours), rather than a yes or no answer. They came to me as 'wishes and wants.' Here are my '40 wishes.'
>
> 1. I want to work with you in the garden, see the sweat come on your brow, and watch you sleep after a hard day.
>
> 2. I want to watch Austin [our grandson] play soccer and root from the sidelines. I want to see your granddaughter dressed as an angel in a Christmas pageant. I want to sit next to you like a proud grandparent.

3. I want to watch you hug my son, as he is dressed in his tux and about to go off to his senior prom.

4. I want to assume a burden of prayer for your children. I will ask God to give them the fullest measure of his kingdom.

5. I want to build or remodel a house together. I want you to teach me everything you can about decorating a home.

6. I want to hike the Scottish moors with you and walk the bonny banks of Loch Lomond. I want to see what the cold weather does to your cheeks.

7. I want to kiss the small of your back.

8. I want to go snorkeling in Anama Bay outside Wikiki.

9. I want to play 97.9 FM music and dance with you until the early hours of the morning (as long as I am home before Scott's curfew).

10. I want to fly to various parts of the world in a 747, holding hands as we sit in the two-seater co-pilot side of the plane.

11. I want to stand by your side as we worship in a British Cathedral.

12. I want to curl up behind you in bed, put my arms around you, and pull you close to me.

13. I want you to take Faye away before her wedding night and tell her how a woman makes love to a man.

14. As we travel and sleep in cold rooms and lumpy beds, I want our presence to make them comfortable.

15. I want to pray in tongues over you as I hold you in my arms.

16. I want to have huge family Christmas parties where everyone knows that Jesus is our best friend.

17. Every time you get in my Suburban, I want to kiss you on the cheek because I am so grateful God has brought you into my life.

18. I want you to lead Meredyth into puberty and teach her everything you know about dressing and design.

19. I want to show you off to all my friends.

20. I want to hold your hand when you bury your mother and for you to be at my side when I do the same with mine.

21. I want to put our feet on the coffee table every Monday night and watch 'Murphy Brown' and 'Designing Women.'

22. I want you to sit with me next year at all of Scott's varsity basketball games.

23. I want to watch the explosions that come from your eyes and explore the crevices of your mouth.

24. I want to watch you come out of the shower, dry your hair, and paint your nails.

25. I want to see you cry, dry your eyes, and be happy again.

26. I want you to have the joy and security of having a spiritual leader as a husband.

27. I want to see your giftedness come alive, seeing you do things that you never thought possible.

28. I want to see your face when I have done something that touches you deeply.

29. I want to live at least 20 healthy years with you.

30. I want us to write a book that will cause grown men to cry, women to swoon, and little children to pray that God would grant them parents like us. I want to write a book that Sheldon Vanuken would envy.[1]

31. I want you at my side when Christian leaders from around the world stay in our 'prophet's chamber.' I want us to sit up late with these folk, absorbing the goodness that is in the people of God.

32. I want you to sit with me in Anne Watson's cottage [York, England], drink English tea and eat scones. I want you to meet Teddy and Margaret Saunders and love a woman who loved Meredyth at a crisis in her life.

33. I want to do London and Edinburgh with you, theaters, museums, and shopping on Princess St.

34. I want Dee to love me and your sons to look up to me.

35. I want to watch you as you reach out your hand to the poor and fulfill all the descriptions of Proverbs 31.

36. I want to take you to Vineyard pastors conferences and let you enjoy the people and the worship.

37. I want to sit arm and arm with you and feel your breast snuggled against the backside of my arm.

38. I want to be there when we both grow old and you wonder if I loved you for more than your good looks and ability to comfort.

39. I want to have a marriage that honors our former mates, shocking people that we could hold such multiple loyalties.

40. Last, if this is not true love, then this will have to do until true love comes along.

I love you. I want you to marry me as soon as it is *sensible*.

Love,
George

(*Carolyn*) As I flew to California, I had numerous thoughts about George and the children. But upon arriving at Jean's, I was consumed with her surgery and recovery. Four days later, when I finally had a chance to call George, I was again shocked by his response on the phone. 'Hi George, this is Carolyn.' His opening words were, 'Sweetheart, sweetheart, I've been missing you so much!' This, no doubt, was the most aggressive man I had ever met. For the next week, we talked every night on the phone. It was in these moments that I really got to see both sides of the man God was bringing into my life. On one hand, he knew what he wanted and was prepared to pursue it, no matter what it took. It was this quality that led him to send flowers one week after our first date, with the inscription, 'One week – the rest of our lives.' Obviously, commitment was not something he was shy about. On the other hand, he knew how to share his feelings and to listen to mine, and our mutual attraction began to grow with each call. As I listened to some of his sermon tapes, I realized that he was a man of God and dedicated to the kingdom of God. Although I was overwhelmed by all this attention, I knew that I would be obedient to God, but that at the same time I was not to be stupid.

Be my Valentine

February 12–16, 1992 (*George*) Carolyn returned from California, and I asked her to give me five days in which to see the inside of my family, myself and the ministry I did. During the week, Carolyn got on her knees in her bed and had a long talk with Hugh. All widows and widowers do this at one time or another, without any attempt to contact the dead or make a theological statement. She just wanted him to know that she loved him, but now she was starting over with me. It was a teary evening, but fully liberating to God's purposes. The rest of the week was lovely, peaking on Valentine's Day when, after presenting her with my letter in a journal, I asked her to marry me.

Although we were enthusiastic about the marriage, as you can imagine, some of our friends and relatives thought we had lost our minds. Thus, we had to tell the story over and over again, assuring people that it was not just 'rebound' on my part, nor a lonely woman on Carolyn's part, that brought us together. I understood the hesitations we were hearing, and would have given the same advice to our friends, but there was certainty about God's leading and we decided to follow that direction.

To some of my close friends I wrote these words:

The personal stages of grief are like personal reading speeds; each of us is on a different page. I do not expect you to be on my page, for you have not gone through nearly four years of 'anticipatory grief.'

From what we have experienced so far, it would appear that my male friends seem to embrace this move faster than my female friends. Yet, every one of you has a concern for me. You don't want me to marry on the rebound and especially to the wrong person. You're worried about my kids and what will happen to them with a new stepmother. I have thought long and hard about these issues, before and after meeting Carolyn, and I am convinced that this direction is the good hand of God. Thus, I hope you can embrace with me the injunction in Romans 12:15, 'weep with those who are weeping and rejoice with those who are rejoicing.'

(*Carolyn*) For the next two months, our lives were consumed with meeting friends and family and getting to know the congregation of the Grace Vineyard. In the midst of these functions, our days were highly romantic. We took picnics in the park, read poetry, and sat for hours gazing into one another's eyes. Our hearts were full of thanksgiving as we contemplated on the goodness of God to call two widows into marriage. Each evening, we knelt by the sofa and prayed together for long periods of time. It was in those hours that a deep spiritual intimacy was born.

April 11, 1992 (*George*) After Carolyn returned from California in February, we began to talk about a date to be married. At one point, we discussed waiting a year or two. But since we had been married fifty-two years between the two of us, we thought it somewhat silly to wait. If the kids would okay it, we would marry seventy days from the day we met, the very day the Lord had given to me in January. Like a soldier preparing for his furlough, I counted the days to my marriage – 'fifteen days and a wake-up.'

The day finally arrived, and we were married in Carolyn's lovely backyard garden.

When Bonnie died, Donna Bromley led Meredyth to the front yard and planted some tulip bulbs. She told her that these bulbs were like the promises of God; though they appeared to be death, they would come to life someday. A few days after I first went out with Carolyn, Meredyth took me outside to see the flowers that were now blooming. I asked her what promises she had requested from the Lord when she planted the bulbs. 'I asked for two things. I wanted my mommy to live forever, so that I could see her someday. And I asked Jesus to give me another mommy real soon.' As I was walking back to the front porch, Meredyth called to me. 'Daddy, guess what? The flowers began to bloom the first day you went out with Carolyn!'

8
THE CHRISTIAN ASSUMPTION

Thus far, Carolyn and I have told our story as simply and truthfully as possible. However, it would be unwise if you should go out and try to recreate our experience, such as deciding to marry someone you have known less than twelve hours, without understanding the assumptions by which we live. Five basic convictions govern the way we think and act.

1. God is alive. Not only does God exist, but he is dynamically present and communicating with his children. Clearly he is beyond our grasp, what theologians call 'transcendence,' but at the same time, he is near to us ('immanence') and knowable.

2. God revealed himself in his Son, Jesus Christ. God consented to make himself known by giving his Son, in human flesh, to the world. By dying on a cross and being raised from the dead, Jesus Christ was acclaimed as the Savior of the world. All history now flows towards one consummate end – the day when every living person will acknowledge that Jesus Christ is Lord.

3. God dwells in the lives of Christians by the presence of the Holy Spirit. The presence of God is more than a faith assumption or a lesson from history. We know his reality by a personal witness which proclaims, 'We are God's children, he is our Father, and his personal Spirit dwells in us.'

The Christian Assumption

4. God's standards for belief and practice are revealed in the Bible. Therefore, ultimate solutions for the problems of life are not found in human wisdom, whether rational or intuitive. Rather, they lie in revealed truth, truth which is above culture and public opinion. This 'true truth' is found in the Bible.

5. Blessing awaits those who walk in obedience to God's revealed truth. Thus, 'no good thing does he withhold from those whose walk is blameless' (Ps 84:11), meaning those who choose to act in obedience to God's direction.

Carolyn and I have attempted to embrace these five assumptions. They color the way we perceive the world and our response to it. We are not always consistent with our beliefs and practices, but to the best of our ability, we 'walk the talk.' In the previous seven chapters, you read our life stories. Now the question to be asked is, 'What have we been taught from our pilgrimage?' In the next five chapters, we spell out the lessons we have learned.

9
TWO LITTLE PILGRIMS, WALKING DOWN THE ROAD OF LIFE

In 1620, a small group of English Puritans left their temporary home in Holland and set sail for Virginia. Winds blew them off course, with the *Mayflower* eventually landing in Plymouth, Massachusetts. William Bradford, the chronicler and eventual governor of the colony, called these new immigrants *pilgrims*.

No doubt, they were called pilgrims for two reasons. First, reflecting on John Bunyan's allegory, *Pilgrim's Progress*, 'they saw themselves as the Lord's soldier-pilgrims, taking uncharted territory and engaging in spiritual warfare. They knew they could not advance one single step, without some degree of opposition.'[1] Second, they were called pilgrims because they were on a journey towards a heavenly city. As Bradford said of them on their departure from Holland, 'So they left the godly and pleasant city which had been their resting place . . .; but they knew they were *pilgrims* and looked not much on those things but lifted their eyes to the heavens, their dearest country . . . and quieted their spirits.'[2]

Much in the same way, the Bible calls people who love God, and long to be with him, *pilgrims*. Precisely, it says that in the quest to know God, they have set their 'hearts on pilgrimage.' Carolyn and I are simply two little pilgrims walking down the road of life. Our story is no more tragic or triumphant than many, but it is a story in which the God of the Bible dramatically revealed himself to be our friend in a time of need. Since we are not particularly special people, we assume that such friendship with God is available to all who have begun the same pilgrimage.

Biographies have a capacity to inspire the reader, but only the dedicated student will plumb the depths of the story to find the principles which sustained the main characters. Carolyn and I want to make this process a little easier for you. We begin by detailing a roadmap of the Christian journey to heaven, developed from Psalm 84. From there we want to give practical help on the themes of suffering, listening to God, and walking by faith. First, let's look at the roadmap.

Heaven bound

> How lovely is your dwelling place, O Lord Almighty!
> My soul yearns, even faints, for the courts of the
>   Lord;
> my heart and my flesh cry out for the living God.
> Even the sparrow has found a home, and the swal-
>   low a nest for herself, where she may have her
>   young –
> a place near your altar,
>   O Lord Almighty, my King and my God.
> Blessed are those who dwell in your house;
>   they are ever praising you (Ps 84:1–4).

In the heart of every man and woman, there is a yearning for the presence of God. There is a deep desire to contact the Mystical, Immaterial and Eternal. Although verbally we may deny this hunger, our behavior betrays us. Mysteriously, we find ourselves moved by poetry or overwhelmed by the creation of a delicate flower. Covertly, we are entranced by a heroic fairy tale or left misty-eyed when real love is portrayed on film. Why? Because eternity is written on our hearts. Our genetic code longs to know God and to be in his presence.

Transparently, the psalmist admits to this basic human need. As a priest of Israel, he sought the Lord in the temple. At the same time, he knew God could not, and would not, be confined to walls built by man. God would then be found, not in a building, but in the hunger of the human heart. *Thus, the purpose of the pilgrimage is to find God and to be enveloped by his presence.*

It's a bumpy road

> Blessed are those whose strength is in you,
>   who have set their *hearts on pilgrimage*.
> As they pass through the Valley of Baca,
>   they make it a place of springs;
>   the autumn rains also cover it with pools.
> They go from strength to strength,
>   till each appears before God in Zion (Ps 84:5–7).

The second section of the Psalm reveals five characteristics of our journey. First, it is a *pilgrimage of the heart* (v5). By definition of the term *pilgrimage*, we are given notice that our journey is a progressive activity, not a one-time event. It will take some time to realize our goal, so we need to prepare ourselves for a long walk, not a short sprint. Each of us is encouraged to join the journey, not to worry about where we are in relationship to other pilgrims. Get in line! Join the procession! Further, the chosen highway for the journey is through the heart. The Bible does not differentiate between the heart and mind, but sees each of us as a unified person, encouraged to give our entire devotion to God. *Thus, the journey will entail giving all of us to all we know of God.*

Second, it will be a *difficult pilgrimage* (v6). Notice the journey passes through the Valley of Baca. To our knowledge, there is no historical place with such a name. Two possible interpretations are commended. 'Baca' could refer to 'balsam trees.' If so, then our journey will pass through arid valleys, desert experiences if you will, where such trees were known to grow. Alternatively, 'Baca' could mean 'weeping.' *Thus, on our pilgrimage we can expect suffering to be in our company.*

Third, if we are to experience some tribulation on this pilgrimage, we need to prepare ourselves with an *attitude check*; '... they make it a place of springs' (v6). What does this mean? Old Testament theologian Derek Kidner captures the essence of this line when he writes; '... a classic statement of faith which dares to dig blessing out of hardship.'[3] Pilgrims, when they pass through the Valley of Baca, will be called upon to dig blessing wells in hardship deserts; *they will be called to transform pain into gain.*

Fourth, the pilgrimage is *blessed by God*. Notice that more than personal effort transforms the desert experience into something profitable; '... the autumn rains also cover it with pools' (v6). Again, what does this mean? When we turn our hearts towards God, embracing his ordained circumstances, he then steps in and adds his own blessing. He brings his rain to supplement the little wells we have dug. *So pilgrims who survive the Valley of Baca are not so much the hearty, but those who faithfully respond to their situation, and God adds his blessing.*

Last, it is a pilgrimage which *takes determination*; 'they go from strength to strength, till each appears before God in Zion' (v7). The Valley of Weeping does not defeat the pilgrim. In fact, *he moves from strength to strength, from his efforts to God's blessing*. 'The nearer the goal, the stronger the pull; so that the pilgrims, so far from flagging, press on more eagerly than at the start.'[4]

Praying for leaders

> Hear my prayer, O Lord God Almighty;
>   listen to me, O God of Jacob.
> Look upon our shield, O God;
>   look with favor on your anointed one (Ps 84:8–9).

This last part of the Psalm is somewhat shocking in its application. Let me put it in my own words. 'Lord, I want to be in your presence more than anything else in the whole world. I know the journey will be difficult. Please *show favor to my leaders*, so that they can enable me to finish this journey.' Where did this idea come from? Verse 9 refers to the 'shield' and the 'anointed one,' both terms used to describe the kings of Israel. In other words, the welfare of the king determines the welfare of the people. *What happens to our leaders will impact our journey towards God*; surely this is a good motivation to pray for those who have leadership roles in shaping our lives; pastors, government officials, and such.

Psalm 84 serves as a good overview to the pilgrimage, but we must press on to answer three practical questions that are posed: How do we handle the pain of the pilgrimage? How do we hear from God as we go along the journey? And how do we have the faith to carry on in the midst of opposition?

10

NO PAIN, NO GAIN!

How long, O Lord, must I call for help?
(Habakkuk 1:2)

Jim and Sue were lovers. It glowed from their oval faces, beamed from their bright smiles and echoed in every word they spoke. They asked me to marry them, and so we began several weeks of pre-marital counseling. I knew Jim as a high-school student and watched him go on to university and to work in France before meeting the girl of his dreams. Both were serious-minded Christians who knew that discipleship to Jesus Christ was not an optional extra for the true believer. All we lacked was one more counseling session before they were married. Tragically, as they were returning from a camping trip, they were involved in a head-on car accident, killing both of them. Jim and Sue were lovers I was to marry; in a matter of seconds, they became friends I had to bury.

Jim and Sue's parents decided to honor the two by having them buried together. Two stately grey caskets lay in front of me as I stood before hundreds of their friends and relatives. I had written out my homily the night before, and as I practiced my delivery, I found myself falling to the floor in tears. Why such a horrible end for this lovely couple? Where was God when they needed him the most? How could I now bring the comfort and faith needed, when the object of our security seemed so hostile to our cause?

Mounting the pulpit, I carried the message of orthodoxy,

although my emotions were less than enthusiastic. 'Where,' I asked, 'was God when Jim and Sue were killed? Where was he when the metal crushed life from their bodies? Where was he when they screamed in terror?' Boldly I asserted, 'He was in the same place when his own Son was crushed and despaired for his life. He was in heaven, watching, and very much in control!'

Twenty years later, that message is as emotionally hard for me to deliver as it was the first time I said it over Jim and Sue. Since then, I have restated it countless times, either to myself or in public. I said it when Rob was stabbed to death in prison, when Patty was murdered, and when Ian and Linda lost their baby. I said it when Bill and Barbara's boy was hurt in a car accident and when Nancy and others told me of the abuse they suffered in their childhood. Over and over I have said it, and the more I see of life's tragedies, the more I believe it to be true. God sees all and is in control of all.

Everyone must deal with the problem of personal suffering, whether we are religious or not. We naturally understand why bad things happen to bad people, but the question remains, 'Why do bad things happen to *good people*?'[1] The answers Carolyn and I suggest may not ease your pain, like they have ours, but they are reasonable and have been of comfort to Christians for generations.

Everyone gets a little rain sometime

Life is not fair, and everyone will suffer some level of trauma. Each of us, particularly in our youth, has an innate sense of fairness. If we do good, we should have good in return, and if we do a little bad, we should suffer only a little. That's the way life is supposed to work! But as we mature, we find that life does not deal proportionally with our behavior. The divorced single-parent, living at a substandard level, loses a hemophiliac child. This deserted, destitute woman produces a genetically-defective child and loses the only thing that makes her

No Pain, No Gain!

life rewarding. Fair? Not in the slightest! The pain-free life is a fairy tale, known only in imagination. Like it or not, that's the way life is, and if we are going to have any hope of a reasonably successful life, we need to acknowledge this fact.

Chances are, if you are reading this book, you know the pain of life and want to know what to do about it. But remember, you have friends who have no idea that life can be painful, and they are about to encounter something which will overwhelm their lives if they are not prepared for it.

The source

Knowing the source of trauma will not automatically resolve personal pain, but it will give a perspective for handling suffering. An out-of-state pastor called with an unusual request. He was very emotional as he described his dilemma. A distant relative had just married and the new couple had gone to Central America for their honeymoon. The day after they arrived, the husband left his hotel room, went across the street, and rented a wind-surfing board. When his wife arrived at the beach some ten minutes later, she saw a crowd surrounding a man lying on the beach. Although there had been no storm clouds, lightning struck the metal rigging of the sail-board, killing the husband instantly. The wife was now returning home, stopping over in Dallas, and the pastor wanted me to care for her on her arrival.

However, as we discussed what happened, the pastor kept asking questions about the source of such catastrophes. I repeated to him what I have said many times before to others; *if you do not have an answer for suffering before the event transpires, you are not likely to have one in the middle of the crisis.* Every person needs to have their own answer for personal tragedy.

What's your answer? Why do bad things happen to good people? And how do *you* resolve the theological and emotional tangles that come with suffering? Let's consider a few options.

The classic statement of the tension goes this way: 'If God allows suffering in the world, he must either be not all powerful, or not all good.' To this assertion, the Bible declares that God is King of the earth, perfectly good and absolutely in control of his universe. So, why the suffering? Two answers, at this juncture, point us in the right direction.

C. S. Lewis once described suffering as 'God's megaphone to arouse a deaf world.' In other words, *suffering grabs our attention like nothing else*. Immediately, we stop in our tracks, take stock of ourselves, and set purposeful resolutions. Without suffering, we would conveniently ignore any intrusions, pursuing only our selfish gain. The world however, as designed by God, is theocentric. God is in the center of everything; he is the source and direction of our lives. Man's choice of rebellion against his Creator changes that focus, making it anthropocentric, centered upon the interest of man. Graciously, God will not let us plunge headlong into this obsession with ourselves. Through the means of suffering, God shouts that we are going in the wrong direction; life is not about us and what we want, but about him and what he wants.

When we think theocentrically, we then understand that this world, and our existence in it, is not all there is. Jesus spoke of a life beyond this one in which rewards and responsibilities would be measured by our stewardship on earth. So to measure success in this life by how long we lived, or how prosperous we were, indicates our failure to comprehend the end for which we were intended. We were sent to serve God, not for him to serve us. Losing Jim and Sue was painful, but to never see them again would be more so. They were faithful disciples, doing what they were given to do, until Jesus called them home. They accomplished their mission, and now they are enjoying the benefits of their faith.

No Pain, No Gain!

There is, however, a second window in this God-centered equation. *The Bible maintains that God has a personal enemy.*[2] This enemy is a fallen angel, who in his rebellion, has gathered about him a host of evil spirits. Their intention is to make war on God's people and to destroy God's world. This mystery of evil is laced within the universe and, by the permission of God, it is allowed to exist. Why God, in his sovereignty, allows his own people to suffer at the hands of this malevolent creature can only be answered one way: *the martyrdom of God's Son and his saints hastens the day evil will be completely destroyed.* So the war rages and the casualties mount, yet the direction of the battle is certain. The death of Jesus dealt a shattering blow to the enemy, and now he has begun to scatter. The final mopping-up operation is at hand.

Therefore, suffering lies at the heart of the biblical drama of redemption. God is retaking his world, and there are casualties on our side, but a righteous victory is assured. Certainly, there are moments when the soldier in the battlefield is confused by the strategy of the General, yet the Commanding Officer has the overall view of the battle and knows the cost of an ultimate victory.

How do we emotionally process this perspective on suffering? Independent of one another, Carolyn and I came to the same conclusions, as we experienced the death of our mates. Did *God* take our mates from us? Yes! Was the *enemy* somehow involved in the process? Yes! Did God allow the enemy *an apparent victory* in the situation? Yes! Does God have a *bigger plan* in mind for us? Yes! Do we *know what it is*? No! Do we have to *live by faith until we know the plan of God*? Yes! Did we have an opportunity to *blame God* for what he allowed in our lives? Yes! Did we *blame God*? No! Why not? Because we had seen his power and love so often in the past we were convinced that he was lacking in neither when he took Hugh and Bonnie home. Was it *hard to accept suffering from God's hand*? Yes! What *made it easier*, if anything? It was made easier by the confession Carolyn and I made when we first became Christians. Jesus Christ is our Lord and we pledged to follow him anywhere and into any experience he might lead us through. Was the *grieving process hard*? Yes! Would we want to *go through it again*? No! Might we have to go through some hard times in the future? We don't know!

Behind the scenes

In spite of our suffering, God is always working behind the scenes, arranging the players and circumstances to his liking and for our benefit. When Jesus died on the cross, hardly anyone expected the resurrection. It appeared that tragedy had won the day. The Good One, moral and helpful when alive, was now ignoble and defeated in death. But God clearly had a surprise in mind all along. He would raise his Son from the dead, in order that he might defeat the enemies of his kingdom.

The Bible suggests that God constantly repeats this same pattern in the lives of his believers. As they walk down the road of life, doing good and having influence, the enemy plots to do them harm. Sometimes, with God's permission, he is even allowed to take their lives, as he did with Hugh and Bonnie. But, always in the mind of God, there is a plan for triumph. The little pilgrims may be wounded and confused, but they will not be defeated. Carolyn had no idea that while she was grieving over Hugh's death in March of 1987, God was calling me home to Texas. And the day I knew Bonnie would die in May of 1988, God was already speaking to Carolyn about marriage to me, although it would be three and one-half years before we met. Life is a drama, and God is the Director. He calls the shots, and we respond in our parts. When we play the part the way he directs, we see the significance and even the beauty of his production.

Embracing life's pain

Whenever pain comes our way, it must be embraced, not denied. Knowing theologically the ins and outs of

No Pain, No Gain!

suffering does not resolve the pain that follows in the wake of the suffering. To be released from this pain, it must be embraced and redeemed.

Prior to Bonnie's death, I found it easy to deny the emotional feelings I had about life. I knew them intellectually; this was anger and that was sorrow, but I was not able to experience them. I was plugged like a dam. As her death grew near, enormous internal pressures began to build up. Soon I was experiencing something quite unusual; I was not in control of my emotions. The pain was too great and I could no longer hold it back. Although the emotional release was well needed, it was at this time that I also realized what the enemy was doing to me. As I grieved, I felt he was holding a spear to my chest. Daily, like a school-yard bully, he threatened me with Bonnie's impending death. He tempted me with words like: 'You won't make it when she is gone! Life is over for you! It's your fault she is dying! God's no longer on your side!'

One day, I got tired of the intimidation and took the challenge head on. *I decided to fall on the enemy's spear, as painful as it was, to find out if by embracing the pain, God would raise the dead.* In those moments I cried out to God, 'It's alright Lord, I accept what you have dealt me. I do not understand why you gave this to me, but I receive it as a gift from your hand!' With that confession, I felt alive again. The fear and the hassel were gone. Now I know that only when pain has penetrated our hearts, when we have embraced the will of God for our lives, can we be fully healed. Only then do we know for sure what it means to be raised from the dead.

Embracing the pain also means to see suffering through God's eyes. Clearly, life is not fair, but God is still good and he is in control. I cannot prove that to you, but I can show you where the Bible tells us that, 'no good thing does he withhold from those whose walk is blameless' (Ps 84:11). Carolyn and I have seen this in practice. To confess the opposite by believing that God is indifferent or even opposed to us leads only to emotional chaos and actually distances us from God. Therefore, crisis invites an opportunity to confess our faith. 'God is good. God is in control. No good thing will he withhold from me.' Such a confession does not change our situation, nor instantly alter our emotions, but it does transform us. When we are pliable clay in the hands of God, he can do with us what he chooses. Notice in the next section how Carolyn processed this very theme in her own life, as she remembered the words of an old familiar hymn shortly after Hugh's death.

Potter and the clay (*Carolyn*)

> Have thine own way Lord! Have thine own way.
> Thou art the Potter, I am the clay.
> Mold me and make me, after thy will.
> While I am waiting, yielded and still.[3]

The night of the accident, this hymn came to mind. I had always loved it, and although I couldn't recall all the lyrics, the opening two lines kept repeating in my brain like the echo of a peaceful refrain. As the days and weeks passed, the melody remained. 'Thou art the Potter, I am the clay.' Without knowing exactly when, I became the clay on the Potter's wheel. It began when I confessed to myself that the only place to be truly secure was in God's hands.

Hands have always been important to me, so expressive, powerful, creative and helpful. My father had wonderful strong hands, and Hugh had the most beautiful large hands I have ever seen. I was lost without those secure, loving hands because they were always holding mine. The first night after his death, I got into our king-size bed alone, and I cried out to the Lord for the comfort of those strong hands. Then, in an unexplainable way, I fell asleep feeling Hugh's hand engulfing mine! What a special grace from the hand of God to me.

As I reflect back over the years, I can see how the Potter has shaped me on his wheel all along. First and foremost, I realized that *God always uses the right clay for the right pot*. Our heritage, values, personality, character, gifts, interests, physical build, temperament and moral fiber make up the clay which suits the purpose the Potter has for our lives.

The first time I fully realized this was after I had completed my five years in Bible Study Fellowship. One day, I received a call from the teaching leader, and she asked me if I would go to a design college in the city to teach a Bible study. It was a two-year college with students from all over the world. After talking with Hugh about this commitment, I knew it was the right thing for me to do, because I was prepared and was sent out with authority and blessing. Soon after the study began, I could see why God had placed me there. To some, the bizarre make-up, hairstyles and far-out fashion would be too much to handle. But I could totally accept and relate to these girls. Not only did I have three teenagers, but I loved design, art and fashion. Their creative statements didn't bother me because I had experienced some of the same feelings. My gifts, talents and interests gave me common ground to understand and to be understood.

As we grow to trust God to direct our lives, we find that he prepares us to perfectly fit the mold of our calling. The Bible study was not only a blessing to us all, but very fruitful; my relationships with some of the students continue to this day. It was obvious that the clay used was ideal for the pot that was chosen.

Next, *the Potter anchors the pot securely to the wheel*. In order to center the pot, the Potter must throw the clay on the wheel with controlled force. On the night of Hugh's death, I felt my life had turned upside down, and indeed it had. Forcefully, God had centered me on his wheel with my crisis of circumstances.

Further, the Potter always has his hands on the pot as he begins the shaping process. With perfect speed and timing, God was preparing the way for me and my children. How clearly I could trace his detailed preparations for us the year before Hugh's death. How generous was his grace and how encouraging was his word, 'No one is able to snatch us out of the Father's hand' (John 10:29).

As the pot is shaped by the pressure of the Potter's fingers, so was my life. The pressures I experienced in my circumstances exposed my weakness and revealed his strength. The pressure to have an income gave birth to a new business. Because of his pressure, my weakness and fear of public speaking was overcome with the assurance of his faithfulness and resulted in ministry. Even the words you now read are a testimony of his grace and power.

The wheel stops and the pot is cut free. Suddenly, the pressure eased, and there was a new beginning. The business was blessed, and I found freedom from financial burdens and time restrictions. This was a time to rest and reflect – to realize that the pot is fired at high temperatures to reveal its flaws. No one knows where they are spiritually until they go through the fire and have been released.

As the Potter works the clay, he has the option to put the clay aside, or pick it up again. This process only comes by the faithfulness of God. Patiently, each day, he prepares the heart to love, the mind to reason, the soul to obey, and the Spirit to lead. As a baker kneads his dough and sets it in a corner to rise, so God kneads these character traits into our lives. Our circumstances are the perfect conditions for us to rise and fall, and rise even higher, until we become edible bread and usable pots. I always smile when I hear this very honest comment, 'I keep climbing off of the wheel!' Until the clay is ready, the Potter faithfully works it, making it the perfect consistency for the pot it is meant to be. Only the Potter knows when the clay is ready and what form it will take.

One Friday, before company officials came to bring me news of my financial benefits, I was humming my little song, 'Thou art the Potter, I am the clay.' I told the Lord I knew I was on his wheel, and I could see the Potter was at work. But my question was, 'What kind

No Pain, No Gain!   97

of pot are you making of me?' My answer came at noon, when my friends Carol and DeeDee walked in carrying a beautifully-wrapped gift. I was speechless because, after all they had done for us during our grieving moments, I should have been the one giving the gift.

I carefully unwrapped the package to find an incredibly magnificent blue Chinese vase with butterflies and flowers etched into it and six exquisite Chinese children climbing on it. I had seen and admired this beautiful piece of fine art before, but it was an investment piece. I was overwhelmed when I saw this 'pot of clay,' because I knew that, once again, God was showing me his truth.

As I told them about the question that I had asked God and the answer that had been brought by them, my friends and I sat and marvelled at the miraculous weaving of our lives to his purpose. We had shared a moment that would remain with me forever and an unbelievable gift as a daily reminder.

The next morning, I was still recalling with praise the blessed events surrounding the vase. It was then that I realized the Lord was showing me that he saw me as complete, perfect, and lacking nothing. As the words in James 1:2–4 revealed,

> Consider it all joy, my brethren, when you encounter various trials [circumstances], knowing that the testing of your faith produces endurance. And let endurance have its perfect results, that you may be perfect and complete, lacking in nothing. (NASB)

'What do you see here, Lord?' I asked, and in my thoughts I could hear him say, 'I have made an investment in you.' He *had* made an investment in me. He made an investment in the world, and it was at *great cost*. It cost him the very life of his Son, who had endured the shame and shed his blood on the cross of Calvary for my sins (1 Peter 1:18–19). Jesus, the sinless one (2 Cor 5:21), paid the price that was required so that those who believed in him would have eternal life (Rom 6:23; Eph 2:3–7).

He made an investment in me when he filled me with the Holy Spirit and gifted me to be a part of his body, the church. Jesus had spoken from the cross and said, 'It is finished.' He had taken the sins of the fallen creation and established a new dominion, the kingdom of God on earth, as it is in heaven. To this spiritual kingdom, Christ, its King, called forth and prepared his church to be a victorious force, filled with his Spirit and held by his power and grace.

But we have this treasure in pots of clay, and even though we are afflicted in every way, we are not crushed; perplexed, we are not despairing; struck down, we are not destroyed. We do not look at the things which are seen, which are temporal, but we focus on those things which are not seen, which are eternal (2 Cor 4:7–9, 17–18).

Impaired vision

Again, the emotional response of the suffering question is always, 'Where is God when I need him the most?' C. S. Lewis experienced this agony at the death of his own wife.

> Meanwhile, where is God? This is one of the most disquieting symptoms. When you are happy, so happy that you have no sense of needing Him, so happy that you are tempted to feel His claims upon you as an interruption, if you remember yourself and turn to Him with gratitude and praise, you will be, or so it feels, welcomed with open arms. But go to Him when your need is desperate, when all other help is vain, and what do you find? A door slammed in your face, and a sound of bolting and double bolting on the inside. After that, silence. You may as well turn away. The longer you wait, the more emphatic the silence will become. There are no lights in the windows. It seemed so once. And that seeming was as strong as this. What can it mean? Why is He so present a commander in our time of prosperity and so very absent a help in a time of trouble?[4]

No Pain, No Gain!

Corrie Ten Boom had an interesting answer to this question, which she gathered from Psalm 91:1: 'He who dwells in the shelter of the Most High will rest in the *shadow* of the Almighty.'[5] There are times when it seems we are living in supposed darkness, for we do not know why we are suffering, nor where God is in the process. But as Ten Boom points out, the darkness is simply the darkness of the shadow of his wing. We are not abandoned as we suspect; in fact, we are closer than we could imagine. The problem lies in our vision. We are in the darkness of the shadow and too close to focus our eyes without light. Thus, we cannot tell how near we actually are to the heart of God. *And so it is in our seasons of suffering – so close, but feeling so distant.*

11
HE IS THERE, AND HE IS NOT SILENT

> *Write down the revelation and make it plain on tablets so that a herald may run with it. For the revelation awaits an appointed time; it speaks of the end and will not prove false. Though it linger, wait for it; it will certainly come and will not delay.*
> (Habakkuk 2:2–3)

No doubt you have noticed our repeated use of phrases such as, 'the Lord told me,' or 'the Lord said.' In fact, *Hearts on Pilgrimage* would not have been written were it not for the revelations Carolyn and I received. However, depending upon your experience with such claims, you may conclude that we are either emotionally deranged or spiritualists with unusual psychic powers. Neither is the case. Rather, as we said in our assumptions, *we believe that God exists and that he is not silent*. God did not create the universe and leave us to fend for ourselves; he sent his personal Spirit to commune with us and to reveal his will for our lives.

God's nature

Louis Eberly has said, 'God hasn't ceased being Revelation any more than he's ceased being Love. He enjoys expressing himself.'[1] God, as revealed in Jesus Christ, has demonstrated that he is a *communicating God* in several tangible ways; for him to stop speaking would be an act inconsistent with his own nature. The Bible is a record of God speaking, or as J.I. Packer says, 'God preaching.'[2] At *creation*, he communicated within the Godhead about the details of his handiwork (Gen 1:26). In the *garden*, he spoke with our first parents, setting boundaries for their behavior (Gen 2:16f). Before the *flood*, he spoke to Noah and saved a remnant of the human race (Gen 6:13). He then spoke to *Abraham* and called a covenant people, the nation of Israel, into existence (Gen 12). He spoke to *Moses* in the burning bush and led Israel out of captivity (Ex 3). He further gave Moses ten great commandments for life (Ex 19–20). Through the *prophets*, God governed his people, rebuked their behavior and led them out of one trouble after another. God's ultimate revelation came in the incarnation of his Son, *Jesus Christ*. In him, the communication of God became flesh (John 1:14, Heb 1:1–4). Through New Testament *apostles and prophets*, God continued to speak to his church with direction, encouragement, and correction. And finally, to each *believer*, the promise of God's communication continues; 'my sheep hear my voice.' (John 10:27)

God's word, the Bible

Carolyn and I believe in hearing God's voice. *However, we do not believe what we have received is in the same category, or equal to the Bible*. The scriptures, both the Old and New Testaments, are God-inspired, hence the term 'inspiration' (2 Tim 3:16). We believe the Bible was superintended by God in its origination and that his special hand was on the authors, not to override their personalities, but to hedge them about in their thoughts and expressions (2 Pet 1:20–21). Because of the special use of the term 'inspiration,' for it speaks of a unique document, we find it inappropriate to use when we hear God today. The Bible, and it alone, is God's final and exclusive authority for matters of faith and practice.

However, the Bible defines another term for hearing

God. 'Revelation' (1 Cor 14:26, 30) refers to the unveiling of something previously hidden. Thus, by the work of the Spirit, things that are unknown and not revealed in scripture can be made known. For example, the Bible gives us clear guidelines on the necessity of working for a living and the ethics required of both employer and employee. However, it does not tell you if you are to take such a job in Kansas City or London. In those matters, we rely upon the Holy Spirit to give us a revelation, to unveil God's specific plan of action.

During this process of discovery, any 'revelation' we receive from the Holy Spirit must be submissive to the authoritative revelation in the Bible for it to be recognized as truly being from God (1 Cor 14:37–38). Although we may be completely sincere in our listening to God, and think we have heard without error, there is the possibility that we have been mistaken in our hearing. In this life, our hearing will sometimes be partial and imperfect (1 Cor 13:9). Thus the need to constantly test what we have heard with scripture, to see if it is valid or not.

Learning to hear

Hearing from God is a learned process which takes discipline and perseverance. We will not hear everything we want, whenever we want to hear it. But we can learn to place ourselves in such a position to hear God's voice, if he chooses to speak. There are some seasons in which words from God flow like a river. On other occasions, the doors of heaven are slammed shut and 'double bolted from the inside' (C.S. Lewis). God will not be manipulated, only heard and obeyed. At the same time, there are principles by which God does speak and when we apply them properly, we begin to hear the voice of our Father.

Discerning voices

First, every voice we hear is not the voice of God. There are many voices that echo in our heads, for the emotionally sane as well as the unstable. Each voice does not have equal credibility. Some emerge out of damaged emotions and give off fearful and negative signals. These are death voices, destroying the soul and the body. Other voices echo out of our own choice, the internal conversation that selects our greatest benefit in any given situation. Still other voices, evil spirits giving direction for the purposes of another kingdom, protrude out of dark and hollow corners. Such inadequate voices are quickly discernible by scripture and wise pastoral counsel. Whatever revelation you receive, if it is truly from God, it will not be threatened by cross-examination with scripture, nor by the confirmation of pastoral leaders.

Hearing by reading

Second, reading the Bible is the primary method of hearing from God. As we have said, the Bible is a unique form of revelation that is authoritative for all people, in all cultures, at all times. Therefore, in matters of doctrine, personal behavior and guidance, the Bible will be our teacher. But the Bible is more than this. As lovers long to read one another's love letters, so the Christian enjoys reading his love letters from God. In the pages are comfort and counsel, bounded by loyalty and forgiveness.

God spoke often to Carolyn and I through scripture in our time of need. On the night of Hugh's death, the Psalms of David came as great comfort to Carolyn (Ps 18,22). The Psalms also played a determinative role in my thinking about Carolyn when I read, shortly after our first date, 'God sets the lonely in families ...' (Ps 68:6). These words were not manufactured for our own ends, but they provided us with the comfort and direction that comes from familiarity with the Bible.

Since the scriptures are the word of God, we need to constantly read them and familiarize ourselves with their content. It is only out of such a foundation that we can judge whether we have truly heard from the Holy Spirit or not. Recently, a woman came to me with this announcement, 'The Lord told me to end my marriage!' As I examined the woman's situation, it was obvious she had no biblical permission to end the marriage.[3] Her hearing was thus spurious, because she did not know what the scriptures clearly teach on divorce. Only when the Bible is read, known, and understood, are we able to judge the ministry of the Holy Spirit communing with us. If you are not familiar with reading and understanding the Bible for yourself, then you might want to read *How To Read the Bible For All Its Worth*, by Gordon Fee and Douglas Stuart.[4]

An indwelling living relationship

Third, if I am a believer in Jesus Christ, the following benefits are mine: the Holy Spirit dwells in me (Rom 8:1–16), I can hear from God (John 10:1–18), and I can speak God's words to other people (Acts 2:17). These are rather bold claims for anyone to make, but they are *benefits* of having a relationship with Jesus Christ. The average person sees religion as a duty to perform, rather than a relationship to nurture. Still others may believe that Christianity is more personal, but they usually confine their relationship to the first time they met God, or 'got saved.' If they have been tutored in traditional Christian environments, they have been told that they are on their way to heaven, and since God is no longer speaking, the Bible is their only means to hear from God.[5] But a further investigation of the scriptures reveals that God purposes not only salvation for people, but communion with them. That communion is enabled when we have a relationship with the Holy Spirit of God.

Hearing God personally

Fourth, in addition to consistent reading of the Bible, we need to ascertain ways in which God most frequently speaks to us. Each believer has a unique way of hearing God's voice, a particular language suited just for you.

Normally, one of three senses will be used. We will either *see something, feel something, or hear something*. Let me review some of the experiences we have shared in the book to make the point clearer.

Occasionally, God has spoken to us through the use of *visions* (Acts 2:17). Visions are mental images that come while we are awake. They can be either in color or black and white. Sometimes they are still images, sometimes they are moving pictures and this is what the Lord used in Denver to alert me about Bonnie's eventual death. As I described in an earlier chapter, I saw a Jeep going over a waterfall, but it was saved from destruction. Then on closer inspection, I could only see four seats. From the things I had heard previously, I knew Bonnie was going to die soon.

God also uses *dreams* to communicate with his children (Acts 2:17). Dreams, like visions, appear constantly in the Bible as means of guidance.[6] All dreams are not the same, thus, there are warnings in scripture about being led exclusively by them (Deut 13:3–5; Jer 23:25–28). Some dreams flow out of our disturbed conscience, while others are genuine revelations from God. Several years before Bonnie died, I had a distinct revelation (June 11, 1988). In a dream, a woman approached me and said she wanted to be my wife. I cried out to the Lord and said I could not marry the woman because Bonnie was my wife. As we began to dialogue, the Lord told me that he wanted to take Bonnie home with him. I asked why he wanted to do this, and he said that she was one of his 'queens.' I asked about my children and how they would endure the trauma, and he said reassuringly, 'They will have a double blessing.' The next morning, able to remember the dream in detail, I began to process, with the Lord, what I had heard. Constantly, I was given the impression that the dream was valid, and I was going to lose Bonnie.

Sometimes God speaks to us with *words to the mind*. I do not mean by this that we hear the audible voice of God, but the words we hear do not originate with us, but come from the Spirit of God informing our minds.

Quite clearly I heard in my mind the following words: 'I will break you, but I will use you,' 'Go to Arlington, Texas,' 'April 11th,' 'I have taken two weeks off.' Carolyn equally heard, 'You will have a relationship with this man. Not who he is, but who he will be. He will go to the Grace Vineyard. You will marry. You will minister together out of the book.' None of this revelation came out of intense religious behavior on our part. We were simply living out our lives as faithfully as we knew how, reading our Bibles daily, and permitting God to speak to us in any way he wanted.

Can our minds play tricks upon us, so that we hear something wrong? Most certainly they can. I remember one evening driving into the countryside to attend a conference. I was going for the first time to hear the man who would later impact my own ministry, the British renewal leader, David Watson. I did not have specific directions to the meeting place, but I had a general idea, and since the notion of listening to God was new, I decided I would listen to him for my needed directions. As I drove along, I concluded in my mind that God intended me to follow the car in front of me to an unknown destination. Well, as you can imagine, I was five miles in the wrong direction before I repented of my foolish antics. I pulled over to the curb and told the Lord I was lost, but that I would carefully listen to him if he would indeed get me to the meeting. As I listened carefully over the next few minutes, I heard and saw my way to the meeting place.

As we mature in listening to God's voice, we begin to discern the pattern in which he speaks to us, either for ourselves or for other people. When I am ministering in churches, I most often have visions of people I will meet, or at least, the clothing they will be wearing. From that, the Lord usually tells me how they can be encouraged or directed. Recently, I heard the Lord say, 'Guatemala refugee.' He then gave me a vision of a man's face and I had a sense that he would become a Christian. That night, after the vision, I was speaking in a church. I

He is There, And He is Not Silent

asked if anyone present was from Guatemala. No one responded. I then said to the congregation, 'I believe this word is for someone I will meet out in public!' A day later, the man in the vision came into a restaurant where Carolyn and I were eating and sat down with his family in the booth behind us. After the meal, I went back and began to talk to him. He was indeed from Guatemala, working with refugees in Canada, and clearly not a Christian. When I told Carlos that I had seen him in a vision and that God was intending to bless his life if he should begin to seek him, tears of conviction began to flow from his eyes. I encouraged him to read the Gospel of Luke, then directed him to a church where Jesus Christ was honored, and where a team of people had already dedicated themselves to pray for his conversion.

Is this a special gift? No, this is just the pattern God uses with me to minister to people. Other believers hear through other avenues. Glenn hears Bible references that he does not know by memory; Debbie sees angels and demons; Terry has dreams; Joe has impressions. Each has a language system, designed by God for them to hear.

Pray for the interpretation

Fifth, if we are uncertain as to the meaning of what we have seen, heard, or felt, we need to make the interpretation a matter of prayer. What we don't understand, we take back to the Lord, repeatedly if necessary, asking him the answer to the riddle he has posed. For it is the glory of God to pose the unknown, and the challenge of man to find it out (Prov 25:2). Carolyn sought the Lord for over three and one-half years as to the meaning of her revelation. Laughably confused on many occasions, she nonetheless persisted to find out what God had meant. Pray, and keep on praying until you know the meaning of God's revelation to you.

Revelations for others

Sixth, more often than not, the revelation God gives is for others and not for ourselves. The primary goal of revelatory gifts is not for us to have some insight into our own future, but to build up the body of Christ (1 Cor 14:1–5). It is clearly true in my case that I hear words for and about other people long before I hear anything for myself. Although our book suggests that Carolyn and I hear all the time about our lives (and we do hear some), more often God is saying things to us about other people. When this is practiced, revelatory gifts are denuded of their selfish orientation. If you need guidance for yourself about some major decision, and no revelation seems to be coming, then attempt to listen for others, knowing that God will surely tell you what you need to know, when you need to know it.

When God grants us revelation for other people, we need always to act in humility in the way we share the word. This means the revelation we share is always in the interrogative, that is, as a question. 'I think the Lord said this to me for you. . . , Do you think it might be true?' There is no need to force a word down someone's throat just to make us look good. Rather, we should be the first to admit that we could clearly be wrong in our hearing. Timing in giving a word is also essential; we need to know not only what to say, but when to say it. Yes, it may be true, but it may not be needed at this time. In addition, sharing a word with a person also demands the pastoring of the word in that person's life. That is, we need to take some pastoral responsibility in seeing the person live up to the correction, or be aided by the encouragement.

Exercise discernment

Seventh, we need to take care in the words of revelation we hear from other people. As the church comes to the end of the twentieth century, God has released a floodgate of revelation gifts. I, for one, am pleased that such gifts have been welcomed back into the church. But

I am not naive; there is much danger in the exercising of these gifts (Matt 7:15–23).

A woman came to me at a conference with these words: 'The Lord says there is something wrong with your heart. You need to go to a doctor!' I did not know the woman, nor did I appreciate the manner in which the word was given. In fact, all I could do about the word was worry, which I'm sure did my heart no good. What was I to do? I asked the Lord as simply as I knew how to confirm his word with two or three witnesses. If I indeed needed to see the doctor, I asked him to reveal it to me through several other sources. There was not the slightest response from any source. After hearing and giving untold numbers of revelatory words, I have concluded that for us to successfully use the gifts God is giving during these last days we must follow these twelve guidelines.

1. Before any 'prophet,' a person with frequent revelatory words, speaks to a congregation, his doctrine and character should be examined and known by the leadership of the church.

2. No prophet is to be given the status of infallibility. No matter how great their anointing, sometimes they are wrong. The Bible is the only revelation from God that is never wrong.

3. As a believer, I need to read the Bible and wait on the Lord for myself, before I ever listen to a prophetic word from someone else. Prophets are no substitute for seeking the Lord personally.

4. With every prophetic word given to me, I need to exercise discernment as to its truth. I, and to some extent my pastoral leadership, are in charge of the discernment process, not the prophet who spoke the word. Every word needs to be confirmed by two or three witnesses. Has the Lord spoken to you about the rightness of the word? Have you received similar words from other people? If you took this word before the church, would they agree with your response to the word? Several illustrations are helpful at this point.

During Bonnie's fourth bout with cancer, a godly

prophet publicly predicted that she would beat the cancer and live, if she abided in a 'capsule' of faith. How were we to understand that word? Naturally, we wanted to believe what was said, but over and over again the Lord continually told me to prepare for her death. The prophet simply missed the word.

I have already said that there were friends and relatives who thought that Carolyn and I were moving too fast in our courtship and marriage. You may wonder how the principle of confirmation by witnesses worked in our own lives? When Carolyn told me the word the Lord had spoken to her, I immediately told the word to Glenn Terrell, my fellow elder at Grace Vineyard, and to Donna Bromley, Bonnie's best friend. I knew both of them were wise in the ways of God, believing his dynamic word, but at the same time they were not foolish enough to let me do my own thing. Donna summarized it best when she said, 'George, it's awfully fast, but it sounds like it could be the Lord.' Over the next few weeks repeated confirmations came from people who were unaware of what was happening in my life. On the morning I was to announce my engagement to Carolyn, a woman in the congregation came to me before the service. She had had a dream of me standing in a church with my palm up and glowing. A woman's small hand was then placed into mine. Several other women were standing by and asking the meaning of the action. I did not reply. But God spoke to the women and said, 'What George is about to do today, I am blessing.' The member of my congregation then said, 'George, what does this mean?' I then handed her the letter which the congregation was to receive that day, explaining the details of my forthcoming marriage to Carolyn.

The writing and naming of this book came about in a similar fashion. On February 16, I was reading Psalm 84 when the words 'hearts on pilgrimage' leapt off the page. I thought to myself, 'That would be a good title for the book.' Five days later I was in the shower when I heard the following words, 'Hearts on pilgrimage. The agonies of life, the ecstasies of love, and the triumph of the Spirit.' When I got out of the shower I went to my mailbox, having failed to collect my mail from the previous day. Among the correspondence was a letter from a New Zealand doctor whom I had not seen in years. Now on the mission field he included me in his yearly missionary newsletter. At the bottom of the letter he penned the following words, 'The Lord has blessed us this year, particularly from the words of Psalm 84:5, "Blessed are those whose strength is in you, who have set their hearts on pilgrimage."' I was absolutely overwhelmed – three times in less than a week God had confirmed the writing and title of our book.

5. I need to avoid hearing prophetic words from people who have strong emotional involvement in my life, or strong personal opinions on the matter.

6. If the word sounds totally off the wall, especially if there is an attempt to correct you, say something like this: 'Brother, I want to keep my heart open before the Lord to hear from him at anytime. However, I don't think this is his word to me, and I must reject it.'

7. Just because we believe that God occasionally speaks through prophetic revelation, we need not believe that revelation is superior to godly wisdom. The cognitive process is not inferior to the intuitive. Only when the Spirit is not informing and conforming the mind is it to be viewed as inadequate.

8. Whenever you are given a word, have it taped or have someone write it down for you. Go over the material from time to time. Prophecy is something that God fulfills according to his word, not something we fulfill according to our efforts.

9. Remember, it is easy to hear only what we want to hear in prophecy. Hearing the prophecy correctly does not guarantee the right interpretation, and the first interpretation may not be the true meaning. Prophecy

comes in prophetic language.[7] 'Suddenly' or 'immediately' may mean fifty days (Acts 1:4–5; 2:2) or the end of the age (Mk 4:26–29). It may mean anything from one day to three years. 'Now' or 'this day' may mean as long as thirty-eight years (1 Sam 13:1–14). 'Very soon' can mean one to ten years. 'I will' without a definite time designation means God will act sometime in the person's life if he is obedient. 'Soon' was a term Jesus used almost two thousand years ago to describe the time of his return. 'Behold, I am coming soon!' (Rev 22:12).

The promise of patience means that tribulation is coming to produce the patience. The promise of wisdom means that God will allow some problems and situations to arise which are beyond our capacity to solve. The promise of love means that we will be dealing with some unlovable people. The promise of faith may mean that we will be brought to the brink of disaster and in need of a miracle. The promise of building or expanding means that deeper foundations will be laid in our lives. The promise of harvest is a call to dedication, diligence, and response. The promise of a great victory may mean that we will enter a great battle if we are not already in one. The promise of restoration may mean that 'things' will be returned to us, or it may mean that we will be dismantled and put back together one piece at a time. The promise of vision may mean the agony of birthing a vision. The promise of success may mean a series of humbling experiences which set the stage for success in God's eyes.

10. Prophets are bad on telling time. They may see an event correctly but not know when it will take place.

11. Sometimes a prophetic word will be wrong, and you will be hurt in the process. This is particularly true with words about romance, marriage and babies. If you have been undiscerning in the process, then it can produce doubt. However, if you have been as discerning as possible, then do the following:

- Acknowledge the word has not been fulfilled.
- Acknowledge that prophets only speak 'in part.'
- Acknowledge that God still speaks to his people.
- Forgive those who gave you the word.
- Acknowledge that you were not as discerning as you could have been and that God forgives you.
- Be open to additional true words that God would speak to you.

12. When God tells someone to do something, he rarely tells them why, how, who and when. Therefore, personal prophecies, no matter how they are worded, will always be partial, progressive and conditional.[8]

God is alive, and he is not silent. Read the Bible and listen to his Spirit. Discern any words offered to you, but bring a believing heart to every situation.

12
'LIVING BY FAITH IN A FALLEN WORLD'[1]

... but the righteous will live by his faith.
(Habakkuk 2:4)

Carolyn and I had only been on our honeymoon for three days when we received one of those all-too-familiar pastoral calls. One of my old high-school chums was in need; his teenage son was lying near death following an automobile accident. As soon as we could, we made a visit to the hospital. David's parents met us in the hallway and led me into the intensive care unit. His head, which had sustained the primary trauma, was swollen and bruised, and forced oxygen kept him breathing during his deep coma. The doctors had been honest with Bill and Barbara, suggesting there was little chance of David's survival, let alone recovery without brain damage. As I stood there holding David's hand and praying, the Lord assured me that he would indeed live and be okay. It was a fairly strong prompting, but I did not have the freedom to share it with Bill and Barbara, lest somehow I promised them something which would not happen. Several weeks later, however, David came out of his coma and was even able to graduate with his spring senior class.

Carol's case was different. Carol Moberg lived much of her adult life as an alcoholic, until one night when she met Jesus personally. From that moment on, she was a different person, eventually joining the staff of our church as a secretary. One afternoon, someone told me that Carol was not feeling well and had gone to the hospital. By the time I arrived, it had already been discovered that she had cancerous tumors in her lungs. When I entered her hospital room, her eyes were full of alarm. Everything had happened so suddenly. Only a few months before, I had performed her marriage and saw her move into a new home, but now the future was uncertain. Quietly, I prayed for wisdom. As I did so I sensed, as certainly as I did with David, that Carol would *not* live. Suddenly, my job assignment had shifted; I was to prepare Carol for her eventual death. On my second visit, I asked her, 'What do you sense God is saying to you?' When she said, 'I don't think I am going to make it' I responded, 'I think you're right!' From that moment on, we were able to discuss and pray over the issues of death and dying. Within a few weeks, while having breakfast with friends, Carol went to be with Jesus.

With all of the benefits of my religious tradition, it failed to teach me the necessity of conscious dependence upon God's presence. Faith was certainly necessary for salvation (Eph 2:8–9), and 'the faith' had to be defended at all cost (1 Peter 3:15; 1 Tim 4:6), but there was never any urgency for moment-by-moment faith. I now believe this absence was due to a theological conviction that God would not do any wondrous deeds in our midst, since these ended with the apostolic age. Therefore, I can say that I grew up undernourished in faith, sublimating what was lacking with reason and intellect. But with Bonnie's illness and the accompanying demands, I began to learn something of the dynamics of personal faith. Now some will argue that if I had had sufficient faith, as I did with David, and Carol, Bonnie would have lived. But such an argument fails to apprehend the real nature of faith and how it is exercised by the Christian. Biblical faith is docile to the purposes of God, allowing for healing or death, earthly victory or defeat (Heb 11:32f).

God's requirement

> And without faith it is impossible to please God, because anyone who comes to him must believe that

he exists and that he rewards those who earnestly seek him. (Heb 11:6)

The New Testament lists eight specific actions which are said to be 'pleasing' to God; chief among these is faith. How do you understand the concept of 'pleasing God'? Do you see it as a religious demand you must keep? Or do you understand it from an emotional angle with the perspective that God is smiling when we do what he desires? Probably both pictures are accurate; it is something that God requires, so it must be in our tool box, but it is also something which delights God's heart. It gives him tremendous pleasure when we exercise faith.

The verse mentioned above suggests that we have no capacity to please God, except by faith. 'Impossible' means, literally, 'without ability.' No tool in our tool box, except faith, can please God. In other words, more industrious behavior – acting nicer or being more diligent, does not get his attention. Nor is it an issue of showing more emotional concern, such as crying or demanding with a loud voice. Nothing, but nothing, will touch God like faith. If that is so, what is faith?

First and foremost, *faith is not so much a quality we possess, but a relationship which we access*. Faith is to be understood in relational terms, not in degrees of measurement; quality not quantity. It is common to hear, 'I don't have much faith today!' as though faith were like the oil in your car ('I'm a quart low today!'). Rather, faith is seen as relationally coming to God. In fact, the Greek term used for 'comes to' could be defined as 'coming to face' God in an attitude of worship. It means drawing near to God, coming close to his face.

Such a movement of faith entails two elements. First, *we must believe that 'God is,'* that the essence of his character is akin to a verb, and not an adjective. The New American Standard Bible translates this verse (Heb 11:6) literally when it says, 'he who comes to God must believe that *he is*.' Now if you are like me, the first reading sounds incomplete. I want to inquire, 'He is *what!*' But there is no qualifier here, for God is a spiritual person, not just an accumulation of characteristics. It is not believing in his goodness, justice, power or mercy; it's believing that 'he is.' Such a statement reminds us of God's revelation of himself to Moses, where God referred to himself as the 'I am' (Ex 3:14). Possibly Moses thought, 'I know that you are, but what are you?' Likewise, the author of Hebrews has something specifically in mind when he uses the present tense verb 'he is', instead of an adjective (e.g. good, powerful). He is saying that *when we come to God, we are to believe that he is dynamically present, existing in heaven and in our midst*, transcendent and immanent.

Therefore, to put a smile on God's face we need to believe that *God is*, not just that *he was*, or even that *he will be*. Most certainly Christianity possesses a historical faith in the death, burial and resurrection of Jesus Christ, but our faith is more than God's work in history. At the same time, we believe that Jesus Christ will soon come again, so we believe in the God of the future, the One who shall be. But having historical faith and a hope for the future return of Christ are not what I am describing. *Faith is believing that God is dynamically present at this moment, in our world and in our lives.*

Now imagine for a moment what you would have done if you had been Carolyn or myself. How would you respond if suddenly you had no means of financial support? How would you respond if sickness took your spouse away? How would you go about finding another wife to care for your children and to support you in the ministry God has given you? Hopefully, you have seen from our story that it was not unusual Christian character that saw us through these traumas, for we are not heroic in the least. Rather, we had both come to believe, long before our crisis of circumstances, that we could access the dynamic presence of God through faith. This did not mean that we always had a sense of his presence; there were many times when we did not. But we did have the conviction that his apparent absence was purposeful, and that shortly, he would reveal his hand in the matter. We confessed that he was present, even when we could neither feel him nor hear anything from him. This position then set the stage for him to speak to us when the time was right.

Accessing the presence

Accessing the dynamic presence of God is not a matter of climbing up into heaven to secure God's attention, nor is it trying to pull Christ down to earth to have him do our bidding. Rather, we begin by understanding each member of the Godhead and his particular function in the purposes of God. Historic Christianity is Trinitarian. We believe that the Father, the Son, and the Spirit are one God with one substance, revealed in the three persons. The Father is in heaven ruling and reigning, while the Son is at the Father's side interceding for us on earth (Rom 8:34). The Holy Spirit lives within us, revealing to us the wishes of the Father and the Son (Rom 8:26–28). So accessing the presence of God begins by listening to the Spirit of God within us, so that we might know the will of God.

How do we access the presence of God through the Holy Spirit? First, we must *affirm* the indwelling presence of the Holy Spirit. Jesus said in John 14:17 that the Holy Spirit had formerly been *in our midst*; he was in the world of the early disciples, but from the day of Pentecost onward, he would be *in* every believer throughout the world. Therefore, we need to thank God that he has sent the Spirit to be within us and to guide us. There will be times when we sense the Spirit's presence very intimately, while at other times, it will seem as if no one is there. Don't let this disturb you! We are not living by our 'senses'; we are living by faith, the conviction that God is present, whether sensed or not.

Next, we need to *ask the Holy Spirit to speak to us*, teach us, comfort us, and counsel us (John 14:26). His specialty is just this, so invite him to speak to you. Ask him to illuminate God's word, the Bible. Let him point out from the scriptures areas that need correction or wisdom. Remember, God's word is sent to test the attitudes of our heart; as the Psalmist says, 'Search me, O God, and know my heart ... ' (Ps 139:23). Thus, exposure to the 'living and active word of God' will produce both holiness and health (Heb 4:12–13). At the same time, ask the Holy Spirit to speak to you through various gifts of the Spirit, such as visions, dreams, prophecies and words of knowledge.

Third, when the indwelling Spirit begins to speak to you, then *begin a dialogue* with him about things you don't understand or need further revelation about. If you get a picture or a word, continue to speak to the Spirit in prayer, asking him what this means, what portion of scripture it addresses, and what he wants you to do with it. The conversation may not last long, but you can be assured that when he is instructing you, you will know the certainty of his presence and the truthfulness of his words.

Last, in all our hearing, *we need to diminish our emotional involvement and press for more understanding with our minds*. All of us have overactive imaginations which can lead us to spiritual bankruptcy. Listening to the Holy Spirit thus involves a disengagement from our own personal agendas, asking only to know the heart and will of God. In our desperate need, say for a job or even a marriage partner, we can hear things that are not the voice of God.

The rewarder

The second element of faith, from our passage in Hebrews, tells us that we are to believe that God is *the rewarder of those who strenuously strive to seek him*. Personal effort in pursuing the dynamic presence of God is rewarded and the rewards are threefold. First, the reward is simply the nearness of God. Aloneness disappears when God takes up his dwelling in the human spirit. The fears of being cast away and alienated are aborted and replaced by a sense of belonging and security. Second, the reward is the revelation that comes from being near to God. As the Psalmist says, 'Your word is a lamp to my feet and a light for my path' (Ps 119:105). Without such revelation, our behavior would be unrestrained, consumed with our own selfish ambition (Prov 29:18). But now there is a lighted pathway, even in dark valleys. Lastly, future honors will be bestowed upon those who seek the presence of God and obey him. For them, the banquet is prepared and places of honor have already been arranged, with new and glorious assignments now awaiting them (Lk 19: 16–19, Rev 19:9).

'The righteous will live by his faith'

The apostle Paul, quoting from the book of Habakkuk (2:4), acknowledged the priority of living by faith in his letter to the Romans (1:17). In the 16th century, Martin Luther understood the significance of these words and let them stand as the watchword for the Protestant Reformation. When Paul quoted these words in Romans he meant as Luther rightly concluded, that *when we believe in Jesus Christ we are judicially declared to be righteous in the sight of God*. However, when Habakkuk penned his words, he meant that *God's righteous people will act faithfully*.

What does this mean, especially in the context of difficult personal circumstances? First, it means that *we believe God is present with us, no matter how severe our trauma*. The frontal assault of the devil is to convince us that God does not exist, or at least that he is inattentive to our particular concern. Faith declares that God is present in all situations and that nothing escapes his notice. So, in difficult moments, we preach to ourselves and confess to God, 'Lord, I know you are here, and I resist the temptation to deny your presence.'

Second, acting in faith means that *we believe in God's word, whether it has come to us from the Bible or through gifts of the Holy Spirit.* We choose to believe God's word over our own and certainly over the enemy's input. We pray,

> Lord, your word says in Hebrews 13:5 that you will never leave me, nor forsake me. I choose to believe that word over any notion of abandonment or desertion. Your word is the only authority I can trust at this moment. In spite of my circumstances, I know your word never fails to speak truth and is my ultimate help.

As Carolyn once said, 'When we walk with God, we walk where he walks and see from his perspective.'

Third, to live faithfully means to *embrace our God-ordained circumstances in a manner that honors God* (James 1:1–18). Every circumstance is ultimately permitted by the hand of God, issuing only one question, 'How will you receive what you have been given?' Bitterness and anger are the pathways to frustration and death, while submission and humility provide for redemption and life. To curse your circumstances is to miss what God intends for your life. Again we pray,

> God, I want to honor you in the way I receive this trial. I bow before you in it. You are the Lord and King of my life. You know what is best for me and the way my life has been chosen for your glory. Now grant me the inner strength, and the resources of a biblically-informed mind, to process the consequences of my life.

Last, to live faithfully means *to walk in obedience to the voice of God.* What he says is what we will do, whether the cost is great or small, for we have been called to be his obedient servants. 'We are unworthy servants; we have only done our duty' (Lk 17:10).

13
OVERS

CAROLYN AND GEORGE

In the childhood game of jacks, 'overs' are permitted (you get the option of a second throw). This is a good metaphor for the way we view our first year of marriage. In our previous marriages, we had between us, fifty-two years of faithfully living with one person. We married Hugh and Bonnie when we were young and immature, thus we went through our fair share of learning experiences – raising children, making a living, and trying to love one another. In retrospect, we could have done a better job with them had we been more motivated and educated, but we didn't know what we didn't know.

Now we have a chance for 'overs,' and we sincerely want to do a better job. Our first year has been full of adventure and high romance, with only a few stressful moments. We have had to work as in all new marriages, but this effort has also allowed us to develop some new values, practices, and family mottos. From this sample, you will get the drift of how we have been doing and how we are planning for the future.

'Don't sweat the small stuff, and remember everything is small stuff.' Nothing is worth an argument; we would rather switch than fight.

'I came to play.' There is no time-off in marriage; every person must be consistently contributing to the relationship.

'**The problem is the problem, the person is not the problem.**' Let's work for the correction of the problem so we both can be happy, rather than wasting our time trying to assess blame.

'**Life is too short to be wasted.**' We are on the downhill now, so we want to savor every minute we have – with our children and grandchildren, with believers, and with each other.

'**Why worry when we can pray?**' God has met our needs at every turn, so we have decided to give up worrying about everything. At least we are going to try, and try again when we fail.

'**Go ahead and fall on the spear!**' We don't know what the future holds for us, but we will embrace the pain and the gain, believing that God's hand is never lifted from our lives.

'**Doing the Moses' shuffle.**' Whenever God gives direction for our lives, more than likely we will resist a little, but we will do what he wants.

'**Kick butt now and take names later.**' We have seen all that is promoted us 'the Christian life,' and we don't mind saying where we disagree. It's one of the benefits of growing older.

'**Man cannot live by bread alone, but by every word that proceeds from the mouth of God**' (Matt 4:4). Hearing God is the only thing that keeps us balanced and healthy. If he does not speak it, we are not going to do it.

'**If God intended sex only for the young, he would not let us live so long.**' This needs no explanation; it speaks for itself.

'**Raising teenagers is real and good, but it's not real good.**' Who needs the Holy Spirit to point out your flaws, when we have a house full of teenagers? Surely God has a sense of humor about this; it would be cruel and unusual punishment if he did not. God love them, they will have their own some day.

'**Its *deja vu* all over again** (Yoggi Berra).' Problems have a way of recycling themselves. The earlier you learn to cope with problems, the better off you will be.

'Who died and left you in charge?' Being bossy with people never gets you anywhere, especially in a family.

'Jesus, the sweetest name I know.' Without him, life would be impossible.

Notes

Chapter 1
1 Oswald Chambers, *My Utmost For His Highest*, (Westwood, N.J.: Barbour and Company, 1963), p 20.

Chapter 2
1 I said these words, unaware that Robert Schuller had a book by that exact title. *Life Is Not Fair, But God Is Good* (Nashville, Tenn: Thomas Nelson, 1991).
2 Murray J. Harris, *From Grave To Glory*, (Grand Rapids, Mich: Zondervan, 1990).

Chapter 3
1 Nineteen months after Hugh died, Carolyn met and spent two hours with Hannah Hurnard, the author of *Hinds' Feet On High Places* (Wheaton, Ill.: Tyndale Publishers, 1986).

Chapter 4
1 Much of this chapter is contained in *Power Encounters In The Western World* (San Francisco, Ca.: Harper and Row, 1987) edited by John Wimber and Kevin Springer.
2 A brief account of this renewal is contained in my book *Furnace of Renewal* (Downers Grove, Ill: Inter-Varsity Press, 1981).
3 *Those Controversial Gifts* is available through Grace Vineyard Christian Fellowship, Box 121012, Arlington, Texas 76012, USA.
4 The full story is recorded in Jack Deere's *Surprised By The Power of the Spirit* (Grand Rapids, Mich.: Zondervan, 1993).

Chapter 6
1 Terry and Shirley Law, *Yet Will I Praise Him*, (Tarrytown, New York: Chosen Books, 1987).

Chapter 7
1 Sheldon Vanuken's *A Severe Mercy* was used by God to soften my heart and to give me courage to live, long before Bonnie became sick.

Chapter 9
1 J. I. Packer, *A Quest For Godliness* (Wheaton, Ill.: Crossway Books, 1990), p 22.
2 Mark Noll, *A History of Christianity in the United States and Canada* (Grand Rapids, Mich.: Eerdmans, 1992), p 38.
3 Derek Kidner, *Tyndale Old Testament Commentaries: Psalms 73–150* (Downers Grove, Ill: Inter-Varsity Press, 1975), p 305.
4 Ibid., p 305.

Chapter 10
1 Rabbi Kushner has attempted to answer this question in his book *Why Bad Things Happen to Good People* (New York, N.Y.: Avon Books, 1981). Kushner fails in his answer by neglecting the reality of a personal Devil who deceives and destroys people.
2 For a fuller description of my reflections on this subject see *Arming For Spiritual Warfare* (Downers Grove, Ill: InterVarsity Press, 1991).
3 'Have Thine Own Way, Lord', words by Adelaide A. Pollard (1862–1934).
4 C.S. Lewis, *A Grief Observed* (London: Faber and Faber, 1966), pp 7–8.
5 This illustration is found in Margaret Magdalene's *Jesus, Man of Prayer* (Downers Grove, Ill.: InterVarsity Press, 1987), p 147.

Chapter 11
1 As quoted in Peter Lord's *Hearing God* (Grand Rapids, Mich: Baker Book House, 1988) p 9.
2 See J. I. Packer's *God Has Spoken* (London: Hodder and

Stoughton, 1965) for an expanded treatment of revelation and the Bible.
3 See Matthew 19:1–8, 1 Corinthians 7:1–16.
4 Gordon Fee and Douglas Stuart, *How To Read the Bible For All Its Worth*, (Grand Rapids, Mich.: Zondervan, 1982).
5 I have argued against such theologies in my book *Those Controversial Gifts*, now available through Grace Vineyard Christian Fellowship.
6 See Genesis 37:5f, Numbers 12:6, Daniel 2, Joel 2:28, Matthew 1:20 and 2:12–22.
7 Much of this material is found in Bill Hamon's, *Prophets and Personal Prophecy* (Shippensburg, Pa.: Destiny Image, 1987).
8 Ibid., pp 145–154.

Chapter 12
1 This title comes from the musical tape *Long Line Of Love*, written by Robin Lyle and Robert Noland (Urgent Records, 1990).

To contact the conference ministry of George and Carolyn Mallone write:

Box 121012
Arlington, Texas 76012
USA